A PRIMER OF HINDUISM

A PRIMER OF HINDUISM

J. N. FARQUHAR

SECOND EDITION REVISED AND ENLARGED

GYAN

Published by

Gyan Publishing House
5, Ansari Road
Daryaganj, New Delhi-110002
Phone: 011-47034999, 9811692060
E-mail: books@gyanbooks.com

Distribution Network
gyanbooks.com
India, USA, Canada, UK, Australia, France

ISBN : 978-81-212-3919-6 (PB)
First Published, London, 1904

2nd Impression 2020

Printed at: Gyan Press, Delhi.

A PRIMER OF HINDUISM

BY

J. N. FARQUHAR, M.A.

LITERARY SECRETARY, NATIONAL COUNCIL OF YOUNG MEN'S CHRISTIAN ASSOCIATIONS, INDIA AND CEYLON

SECOND EDITION REVISED AND ENLARGED

ἀνακεφαλαιώσασθαι τὰ πάντα ἐν τῷ Χριστῷ

HUMPHREY MILFORD
OXFORD UNIVERSITY PRESS
LONDON, NEW YORK, TORONTO, MELBOURNE
BOMBAY AND MADRAS
THE ASSOCIATION PRESS, CALCUTTA
1914

PREFACE

It is the conviction of the writer of this *Primer* that Hinduism cannot be understood unless it be studied historically. For this reason the first thirteen chapters of the book deal with the growth of the religion in connexion with the political and literary history of the country. Only when the student has realized how Hinduism came to be is he in a position to attempt to study any particular part of the religion. To think of the religion as a sort of intricate machine to be studied in pieces is to misconceive the whole.

The practical purpose in view has dictated the method of teaching the history. The long millenniums have been divided into periods, so that the mind may be able to retain the course of events. But it is most necessary to realize that these divisions are artificial, and that, while they do correspond to changes, they must not be pressed too far. There is usually no hard line between the periods: one melts into the other.

The exact dates of most of the events in the history of Hinduism are unknown, and the same is true with regard to the literature. But, although the dates are unknown, the order of events, and the relative age of the great groups of books, and of many of the individual books, are well established. For this reason the general place of certain events and books is often indicated in the tables of this *Primer*, even when no definite dates are available.

The Illustrative Readings will, it is hoped, enable the reader to envisage the character of the leading books more vividly than is possible from a bare description. The tables are meant to bring chronological and other relationships before the mind in concrete form, and to serve for reference.

CONTENTS

LIST OF ILLUSTRATIONS

PART I

OUTLINE OF THE HISTORY OF HINDUISM

CHAPTER I

PREHISTORIC PERIOD

1. **(A) The Aryan People.** In the dim background of history we catch misty glimpses of a great people which had a common culture, a common religion, and a common language, but which in the following centuries through division and migration split up into many groups and thus produced a large number of the leading nations of Europe and of Asia. In the language, religion, and life of their descendants we can still find traces of the common life lived so long ago by the Aryan race.

2. The careful comparison of the religions of the various ancient Aryan peoples enables us to realize in some degree what the religion was in the still earlier days of the undivided people. It seems certain, first of all, that they honoured a vast number of special gods, each of them supposed to oversee some distinct aspect of life. But in that primitive age these Aryan men had already another group of gods distinguished as the heavenly ones (*deva—deus*) from the vulgar throng. They were all natural phenomena, but they were

NOTE.—The head-piece above is part of the coping of the rail of the Bharhut Buddhist Stūpa now in Calcutta Museum (Cunningham, *Stūpa of Bharhut*, pl. xlii). See below, p. 62.

also all connected one way or another with the sky and with the grandest of nature's operations. It seems clear that the undivided people already worshipped Sky, Sun, Moon, Dawn, Wind, Fire. But though they regarded and worshipped them as gods, they still called them by their significant names; they had not given them proper names or epithets. The usual method of obtaining the help of the gods in those days seems to have been already prayer and sacrifice of a rudimentary kind. In both prayer and sacrifice true religious feeling mingled with belief in the occult power of charmed words and deeds. It was believed that special knowledge was required for both prayer and sacrifice. Hence, the man of skill in these important matters was a person of consequence. The Latin word *flāmen* and the Sanskrit *brāhman* seem both to go back to the Aryan original which was used to designate this embryo priest. The earliest form of sacrifice consisted merely in laying out food and drink on the ground for the gods to come and enjoy.

3. Ancestor-worship was almost as important to the original Aryan people as the worship of the gods. Uncivilized people usually believe that the soul survives death and lives a new life apart from the body. But early man, not having been able to reach the idea of spirit as distinct from material substance, conceives the soul as a material thing, and believes that after death it is dependent for its continued existence on food and drink precisely like a living man. In consequence of this, nearly all primitive races have been accustomed to provide food and drink for the departed souls of members of their own family. The food is laid out as for a feast, and the souls of the dead are invited to come and eat and be nourished thereby. We must note carefully that this practice, which is all but universal among the simpler peoples, is a service of souls

and not a worship. The dead are dependent on the family for their nourishment.

4. But these beliefs have passed among many peoples into a more developed stage, where the dead are conceived as being powerful beings, controlling the welfare of the family. When this idea arises, the old service of the dead becomes a worship. The family pays them great reverence, not merely because they are relatives, but in order to secure their loving care over the family. This form of worship, then, had been developed before the original Aryan race split up.

5. The father was the high-priest of the family, and controlled the worship of the ancestors of the family in all details. He alone knew the peculiar ritual which was traditional in his family, and which had to be maintained unchanged, if the favour of the dead was to be retained. He alone had the power to pass on the rites to his son. As high-priest of the ancestral rites he was the acknowledged head of the family. The reverence and the power which his priestly position brought him made him supreme in the home. He had full power over his wife and his young children, and in many of the nations of a later date his grown-up sons also were completely under his authority. The property of the family was altogether in his hands. This is the source of the *patria potestas* of Rome, and of the prominent place held by the father in Greece, Persia, India, and among Teutonic and Slavonic peoples as well.

6. This type of family, which is known as the patriarchal, succeeded an earlier and less developed type; and the changed form of family life produced great and far-reaching results. The first of these was a new consciousness of the unity, sanctity, and value of the family; and this new and lofty conception produced in turn a great advance in family morality, in family feeling, and family pride. Marriage

became universal; for every man wanted a son to take over the worship of the ancestors at his death. Since the father was supreme, and since every family wanted sons, there was a tendency to set less value on woman. In consequence many girl babies were exposed or put to death in every race practising ancestor-worship; and a woman was held to be of far less account than a man.

7. **(B) The Indo-Iranian People.** A certain portion of the mighty Aryan family broke away from the main stock—we do not know when or where—and remained a united people for some time, but finally fell in two, one taking up its abode in Iran, the other moving into the territory on both sides of the upper Indus. This people, the ancestors of the Zoroastrians and of the creators of Hinduism, may be designated Indo-Iranian during the period while they were still one. By inference from the Vedas, the earliest literature of India, on the one hand, and from the *Avesta* and other Iranian records, on the other, we are able to realize in hazy outline what the religion of this prehistoric people was. The *Avesta* is the literature produced by Zoroaster and his friends in the great reformation carried out by them about 600 B.C., but it contains many older elements.

8. Clearly considerable advance had been made in conceiving the heavenly gods; for there is now quite a group of personalized divinities with definite names and lofty functions. It seems clear that the following at least were fully recognized, Varuṇa, Mitra, Aryaman, Bhaga, and Indra, and along with them Yama and Soma. Theology had made a good deal of progress; for they are thought of as spiritual beings, and the natural phenomena from which they originally sprang are now but the medium of their manifestation.

9. The sacrifice, meanwhile, had been greatly elaborated. A ritual had been established, and hymns as well as prayers

accompanied the stated acts. The home of the gods being now consistently believed to be in heaven, it was the common practice to send the sacrifice to them on the flames and smoke of the altar fire. The drink of the gods offered in sacrifice is the juice of a plant called *soma* in Sanskrit, *haoma* in Zend, the language of the *Avesta*. A special ritual for the offering of this divine drink had appeared, and the drink itself had undergone apotheosis. *Soma* is already a god. The priests, too, have now far fuller functions and are called by special names.

10. The belief about the dead had also made considerable progress. Burning had almost universally taken the place of burying, probably from a wish to release the soul as completely as possible from the body and to bear it away on the flame of the pyre to the heavenly regions. For when men die, they are believed to go to heaven, where they join the blessed dead and enjoy immortality with the gods. They are invited to the sacrifices in the same way as the gods. They are believed to be very powerful.

Note.—The tail-piece below is another part of the coping of the rail of the Bharhut Stūpa (Cunningham, *Stūpa of Bharhut*, pl. xliii). Note the animals worshipping the sacred tree. See below, p. 62.

TABLES

1. The Aryan Family of Languages

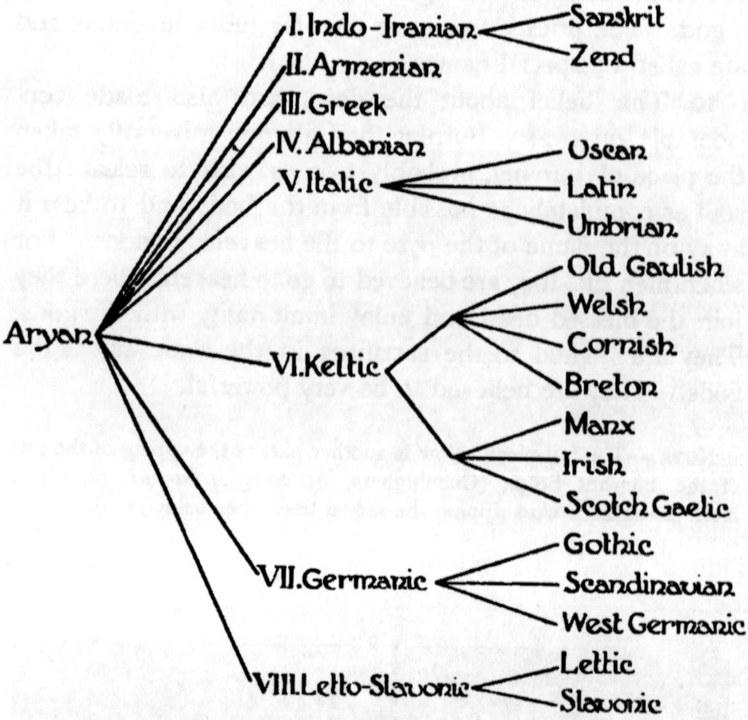

तत्सवितुर्वरेण्यं भर्गो देवस्य धीमहि ।
धियो यो नः प्रचोदयात् ॥

CHAPTER II

CREATIVE PERIOD

THE THREE VEDAS

Dates Unknown

11. *History.* Our first historical knowledge of the Aryan tribes which produced the great civilization of India shows them settled in the Western Punjab and beyond the Indus. They were a tall, fair people. They gradually spread further east, as far as the district of Karnāl, later known as the holy land of the Kurus, Kurukshetra. They were then soldier-farmers, equally used to the plough and the sword. They were constantly at war with the aborigines around them; and they looked eagerly for sunshine and rain to mature their crops and give them fodder for their cattle and herds. They were still a primitive people, living in simple villages, with but few of the arts of civilization, and untrammelled by the bonds of caste. They had no writing and no coinage. They ate beef and drank intoxicating drink. The tribes lived each under its own chieftain, and

NOTE.—The text at the top of the page is THE GĀYATRĪ, the most famous of Hindu prayers: 'That excellent glory of the Quickening Sun, the god, may we attain; may he stimulate our devotions.' *Ṛigveda*, III. lxii. 10.

now and then quarrels led to war among them. The family was still in a healthy condition. Their women had a great deal of freedom throughout their lives. There was no child-marriage among them, no seclusion in the zenāna, no widow-burning, and no law against the remarriage of widows. Like most primitive peoples, they practised the exposure of girl children and old people.

12. *Religion.* Like their early Aryan ancestors, they worshipped the heavenly powers, calling them *devas*; and they were very conscious of the great advantage which their knowledge of these gods gave them over the aborigines. They arranged their gods in three groups, according as they belonged to the upper region of light, the atmosphere, or the earth. These three groups were designated Upper, Middle, and Lower. The chief divinities were—Upper: *Varuṇa, Sūrya, Savitṛi, Vishṇu, Ushas, Aditi, Mitra, Aryaman, the Aśvins;* Middle: *Vāta, Indra, Rudra, Parjanya, the Maruts;* Lower: *Agni, Soma, Yama.* Their worship was largely sacrificial. Animals were often killed in sacrifice; but their most elaborate rites were connected with the offering of the *Soma*, of which we have already heard, and of clarified butter, called *ghī*. They were accustomed to have hymns recited at all sacrifices. But, although they laid so much stress on sacrifice, they had no temples and no images. Sacrifices were offered in the open air, and the arrangements were very simple. The gods were so closely connected with natural phenomena that no visible symbol was required.

Already the people seem to have been roughly divided into three groups—warriors, priests, and agriculturists; but they were classes rather than castes. The priest, Brāhman, was already very influential; for he was believed to have great power over the gods. Every chieftain had his own Brāhman chaplain, *purohita*, whose help he sought before entering on any undertaking. The priests tended to become a caste; for they already made great pretensions and claimed exclusive powers. They were sub-divided into three orders,[1] each of which had its own special duties to perform at the sacrifices. Already schools were in existence for the education of priests. In this fact lies one of the chief reasons for the extraordinary predominance which the Brāhmans finally attained.

13. Austerity, called *tapas* in Sanskrit, was practised in those days. Various forms of self-torture were endured, with a view to securing warlike prowess, invincibility, miraculous powers, or heaven. The *muni*, who practised *tapas*, wore yellow robes.

14. The worship of ancestors was kept up with great care by the Indo-Aryans. They were called *pitaras*, 'fathers,' were regularly worshipped, and were invited to come to the sacrifice along with the gods. After death it was believed that the souls of the good were conducted by Yama to the place prepared for them, where they enjoyed an immortality of peace and happiness along with the 'fathers' and the gods. There was no doctrine of transmigration in those days.

15. *Literature.* By the end of this period the centre of Hindu culture had moved east with the moving tribes to the holy field of Kurukshetra. The hymns, which had been composed during the previous centuries, and which were carefully preserved in the great families and believed to be inspired, were now gradually gathered in some priestly school into the great collection which is called the *Ṛigveda*. Young Brāhmans committed these hymns to memory at school, in order to be able to use them at the sacrifices. The collection was universally accepted by the people as their sacred book, every hymn being recognized as a divine utterance revealed to the *ṛishi*, 'seer,' whose name it bears.

[1] See p. 28.

Just ere the collection was closed, a hymn was added which declares that the three great divisions of the people and the aboriginal Śūdras had each a distinct origin in God. Thus a religious basis was found for that old-world form of fixed social organization which soon developed into caste.

16. These hymns which form the *Ṛigveda* are one of the most interesting groups of literature in all the world. No other people ever produced a body of religious poetry of such striking originality and beauty at such an early stage of their history. The nearest parallel is formed by the Zoroastrian *Gāthas* or hymns of the *Avesta*, the earliest literature of the sister people, the Iranians or early Persians; but they have not nearly the interest and power of the *Ṛigveda*. The people in their daily life, their war, toil and worship, stand out clear and distinct in these hymns; and there is something most fascinating in the way the gods are conceived and addressed.

A few of the latest hymns are philosophical. They ask questions rather than answer them; yet already the conception of the One behind all the gods finds expression, and a number of the ideas which afterwards helped to create the Hindu systems are tentatively put forward.

17. At a later date a large number of verses were gathered together, nearly all of them from the *Ṛigveda*, and so arranged as to form a special manual for the second order[1] of priests. This collection was called the *Sāmaveda*. Its verses were chanted at the Soma sacrifice. Another manual, consisting partly of verses, partly of sacrificial formulae in prose, was put together for the use of the third order,[1] and was called the *Yajurveda*. At a later date a new school separated the sacrificial formulae from the verses. The old *Yajurveda* was thereafter called Black, while the unmixed text was known as the White. These new collections were

[1] See p. 28.

held to be divinely inspired, just like the *Ṛigveda*. They were Revelation in the fullest sense. The word for revelation is *śruti*, 'hearing.' When the second and third orders had each formed its own *Veda*, the *Ṛigveda* tended to become the manual of the first order[1] only.

[1] See p. 28.

Note.—The text below is THE CHARTER OF CASTE :—

'The Brāhman was his (Purusha's) mouth ; the Rājanya was made from his arms ; his thighs became the Vaiśya ; from his feet the Śūdra was produced.' *Ṛigveda*, X. xc. 12.

ब्राह्मणोऽस्य मुखमासीद्बाहू राजन्यः कृतः ।
ऊरू तदस्य यद्वैश्यः पद्भ्यां शूद्रो अजायत ॥

ILLUSTRATIVE READINGS

1. A Hymn to Agni, the Priest among the Gods

NOTE.—Fire is one of the early Aryan gods. When it became customary to send the sacrifice to the gods by fire, Agni, the fire-god, became recognized by the Indo-Aryans as the Messenger of the sacrifice, the great Priest.

O worthy of oblation, Lord of prospering powers, assume thy robes, and offer this our sacrifice.

Sit, ever to be chosen, as our Priest, most youthful, through our hymns, O Agni, through our heavenly word.

For here a Father for his son, Kinsman for kinsman worshippeth, and Friend, choice-worthy, for his friend.

Here let the foe-destroyers sit, Varuṇa, Mitra, Aryaman, like men, upon our sacred grass.

O ancient Herald, be thou glad in this our rite and fellowship; hearken thou well to these our songs.

Whate'er in this perpetual course we sacrifice to god and god, that gift is offered up in thee.

May he be our dear household Lord, Priest, pleasant and choice-worthy; may we, with bright fires, be dear to him.

The gods, adored with brilliant fires, have granted precious wealth to us; so, with bright fires, we pray to thee.

And, O Immortal One, so may the eulogies of mortal men belong to us and thee alike.

With all thy fires, O Agni, find pleasure in this our sacrifice, and this our speech, O Son of Strength.

Ṛigveda, I. xxvi; Griffith, vol. i. 34.

2. Funeral Hymn

NOTE.—The verses of this hymn are used in the Hindu funeral ceremony as it is prescribed in the Sūtras. See Āśvalāyana, *Gṛihyasūtra*, iv. 1–6.

Him who departed over the mighty mountains, and thus showed the path to many, the son of Vivasvant, the gatherer of the peoples, Yama the king, do thou honour with an oblation.

Yama first found a refuge for us; nor can that rich land be taken away. Whither our fathers of old time have gone, thither along their own paths the children go.

Go forth, go forth by the ancient paths whither our fathers of old time have gone. Thou shalt see both kings rejoicing in their bliss, Yama and Varuṇa the god.

Go join the Fathers, join Yama, and thy merit in highest heaven. Leaving thy imperfections, return to thy home, and, filled with life, join thy body.

Depart, separate and disperse: for him the Fathers have prepared this place; Yama grants him a place of rest, adorned with days and waters and nights.

By the straight path hasten thou past the two Sārameyan dogs, four-eyed, brindled. Then draw near the mindful Fathers, who revel in bliss with Yama.

And these two dogs of thine, Yama, warders, four-eyed, path-guardians, men-beholders, to them do thou entrust this man, O king, and bestow both health and wealth upon him.

Ṛigveda, X. xiv. 1–2, 7–11.

TABLES

2. The Divisions of the Vedic People which became the Great Castes

1. *Brāhmans:* prayer-men, priests.
2. *Kshatriyas:* authority-men, rulers and soldiers (called also *Rājanyas*).
3. *Vaiśyas:* men of the people, agriculturalists.
4. *Śūdras:* aboriginal people brought under Brāhman authority.

3. The Three Orders of Brāhmans

1. *hotṛi*	= 'sacrificer'	from *hu*	= pour on the fire.
2. *udgātṛi*	= 'singer'	from *udgai*	= sing.
3. *adhvaryu*	= 'working priest'	from *adhvara*	= a ritual act.

4. The Vedas and their Names

the *hotṛi*	recites	*ṛichas*,	'praises':	hence *Ṛigveda*.
the *udgātṛi*	raises	*sāmāni*,	'chants':	hence *Sāmaveda*.
the *adhvaryu*	mutters	*yajūṁshi*,	'sacrificial formulae';	hence *Yajurveda*.

NOTE.—The word *Veda* means knowledge.

5. Growth of the Three Vedas

DATES UNKNOWN

External Events.	*History.*	*Literature.*		
	The Indo-Aryans on both sides of the Indus.	Gradual		
Israel leaves Egypt, about 1320 B.C.		Composition		
	The Priests divided into Three Orders.	of		
Fall of Troy.		the		
	Rise of Priestly Education.	Hymns.		
David, King of Israel, about 1000 B.C.				
	The Indo-Aryans as far east as Kurukshetra.	Gradual Compilation of the *Ṛigveda*.		
	Theory of the Four Castes.		Compilation of the *Sāmaveda*.	Compilation of the *Yajurveda*.

द्वया वै देवाः । देवा अहैव देवाः । अथ ये ब्राह्मणाः शुश्रुवांसोऽनूचानास्ते मनुष्यदेवाः ॥

CHAPTER III

SACERDOTAL PERIOD

THE BRĀHMAṆAS

Dates Unknown

18. The great question which we have to learn to answer at this point is: How did the simple people we have just heard of become the Hindus whom we know? The transformation took place as a result of two forces:—

(*a*) The gradual development of the culture of the people.

(*b*) The gradual conquest of India by them.

The conquest was carried out partly by war, but largely by the priests, who won over the tribes by their superior knowledge and culture. This chapter and the following will show how the simple faith of the *Ṛigveda* was transformed into the Hindu system.

19. *History*. The Aryans continued to advance eastwards during this period, leavening the old population as they went, until by its close nearly the whole of North India had come under their government and civilization. As they

Note.—The text at the top of the page calls THE BRĀHMANS GODS: 'Verily, there are two kinds of gods; for, indeed, the gods are the gods; and the Brāhmans who have studied and teach sacred lore are the human gods.' ***Śatapatha Brāhmaṇa*, II. ii. 2, 6.**

went, the Brāhmans brought the aboriginal tribes under their priestly rule, giving each tribe a definite place in their social system, which was now steadily stiffening into caste. Thus many new caste-groups arose. The land was divided into a great many small kingdoms, most of them ruled by kings of Aryan race. Large trade sprang up; even sea voyages on the Indian Ocean were undertaken; and wealth increased. Through the intercourse of Indian sailors with merchants in Babylonia the art of writing was introduced; but for lack of suitable writing materials it was not used for literary purposes for many centuries. By the end of the period the patriarchal family had become more developed, and women were beginning to be looked down upon. It became the rule that a Hindu could not eat with his wife.

20. *Religion.* The extension and elaboration of the sacrificial system is what gives this period its religious character. While, in the times of the *Ṛigveda*, men sought to win the regard of the gods, or to persuade them to give their help by sacrifice, hymn and prayer, in this new period the sacrifice is regarded as a mysterious operation which, if faithfully carried out, will irresistibly compel the gods to grant the appropriate reward. If only carried far enough, sacrifices will exalt a man to the level of the gods. The accurate performance of every detail of the ritual thus became a matter of extremest importance.

21. For this reason the priest was all-powerful. His help was needed at every point in the intricate ceremonial of the altar. Without him the layman was helpless. Hence the divine authority of the Brāhman was fully acknowledged and became firmly rooted in the religious practice of the nation. Indeed, so great had the power of the priests become that they were spoken of as gods upon earth, and were feared even more than the gods of heaven. Fees paid to them were declared to be quite as meritorious as sacrifices offered to the celestials. All the old sacrifices were greatly extended and elaborated, so that no layman could conduct them with accuracy. It was during this period that the *Rājasūya*, or Coronation Sacrifice, the *Aśvamedha*, or Horse Sacrifice, an assertion of imperial authority, the *Purushamedha*, or Human Sacrifice (but a substitute was used), and the other great sacrifices, took definite form and became famous.

22. During this period the theological ideas of the Brāhmans underwent a great change. A deep tendency is manifested towards belief in one God, either the personal Creator, Prajāpati, or, more often, a mysterious incomprehensible divine essence diffused through all things. Along with this new God came the idea that the ordinary gods were merely mortals until they extorted immortality from the Supreme by sacrifice and austerity. Many of the ancient gods had already fallen into the background, while others had come into great prominence, among whom were Rudra, who now received his more attractive name, Śiva, and Vishṇu; Śiva as the mountain-god and the god of thieves, and Vishṇu as the sun-god.

1. A VĀNAPRASTHA AND HIS HUT
From the Bharhut Stūpa, now in Calcutta Museum (Cunningham, pl. xlvi). See below, p. 62.

23. Towards the end of this period we begin to meet a real order of ascetics. They lived in the forest and usually built themselves huts of wood or leaves. They were called *Vānaprasthas*, forest-dwellers, hermits, and a collection of their huts was called an *āśrama*, hermitage. They wore coats of bark or skin, wound up their hair in matted coils, and lived largely on woodland fare. The law of *ahiṁsā* (harmlessness), that they must not kill an animal nor break a living twig from a tree, gradually arose among them. They continued the worship of the gods and the worship of their ancestors, and they retained their place in the family and in caste, but did no work of any kind. They practised various methods of severe austerity, enduring extreme cold and heat, strange food, most painful postures, and such like. The purpose of the endurance of this *tapas* was still in the main the attainment of miraculous powers; but moral aims now began to mingle with the older motives. Hermits seek purity of soul and nearness to God as well as power over gods and men. A special form of teaching, called *āraṇyaka*, i.e. belonging to the forest, seems to have been given to young men who were about to enter upon the hermit life. The essential element in this forest teaching was an attempt to spiritualize the sacrifice by means of allegory. This instruction would then form the basis of the hermit's meditation in the forest.

2. AN ĀŚRAMA

Two Vānaprasthas with their huts and the implements of fire-sacrifice in a hunting scene from the Buddhist Stūpa at Sāñchī (Maisey, pl. xxiii). See below, p. 61.

24. The aboriginal tribes were allowed to retain their old gods and their old worship. A practical acknowledgement of the supremacy of the Brāhmans and of Brāhmanic ideas was all that was demanded of them. Naturally, in the intercourse which thus sprang up, the aborigines learned much from the Aryans. On the other hand, a great many aboriginal ideas and many alien religious practices and conceptions found their way into the Vedic faith. The most important change thus produced was the movement of thought towards Transmigration. Snakes, trees, and pools were by this time held in great reverence, and pilgrimage was recognized as a meritorious religious practice.

25. *Literature, &c.* The priestly schools had now become great and learned associations, each with a tradition of its own; and so honoured were they that a man was proud to avow himself a member of his school. Every Brāhman had to pass through one of them, in order to qualify as a priest. He had to learn by heart the Veda which belonged to his order, and to receive from the lips of his teacher a great deal of detailed information, especially with regard to his work at the altar, the correct pronunciation of the sacred hymns and the meaning of certain acts and stories. Language-study had made considerable progress among them. As time went on, the teaching given in each school took definite form and was handed down with great verbal accuracy from teacher to pupil. The oral tradition of a school was called the *Brāhmaṇa* of that school. From this point onward then each priest studied the *Veda* of his order and the *Brāhmaṇa* pertaining to it. Then as education advanced, a number of schools arose under each Veda, and differences, great and small, crept into the teaching, until each great school had its own *Brāhmaṇa*, usually called by the traditional name of the school. Thus arose the Brāhmaṇas, the most absurd and uninteresting prose literature in all the world. They are, however, of considerable value historically; for they enable scholars to form a picture of the life and religion of the times.

During this period a fourth Veda, the *Atharvaveda*, was

compiled. Although as a collection it is later than the other three, a great deal of the material embodied in it is of early date. It is a more popular work than the other Vedas, reflecting the superstitions of the people, and consists mostly of charms, which are of two classes, those that bring weal and those that bring woe. It was some time before the *Atharvaveda* received equal recognition with the three older collections.

NOTE.—The text below gives the rule, that A MAN MUST NOT EAT WITH HIS WIFE: 'Hence let him not eat in presence of his wife; for from him who does not a vigorous son is born; and she in whose presence he does not eat bears a vigorous son.' *Śatapatha Brāhmaṇa*, X. v. 2, 9.

तस्माज्जायाया अन्ते नाश्नीयाद् वीर्यवान्हास्माज्जायते
वीर्यवन्तमु ह सा जनयति यस्या अन्ते नाश्नाति ॥

ILLUSTRATIVE READINGS

3. The Origin and the Power of Sacrifice

Now Prajāpati the lord of creatures, having created living beings, felt himself as it were exhausted. The creatures turned away from him; the creatures did not abide with him for his joy and food.

He thought within him, 'I have exhausted myself, and the object for which I have created has not been accomplished; my creatures have turned away from me, the creatures have not abode with me for my joy and food.'

Prajāpati thought within him, 'How can I again strengthen myself; the creatures might then return to me; the creatures might abide with me for my joy and food.'

He went on praising and toiling, desirous of creatures. He beheld that set of eleven victims. By offering therewith Prajāpati again strengthened himself; the creatures returned to him, his creatures abode for his joy and food. By offering he truly became better.

Therefore, then, let the sacrificer offer with the set of eleven victims, for thus he truly strengthens himself by offspring and cattle; the creatures turn unto him, the creatures abide with him for his joy and food; he truly becomes better by offering; therefore, then, let him offer with the set of eleven victims.

Śatapatha Brāhmaṇa, III. ix. 1, 1–5; *S.B.E.* xxvi. 217–18.

4. A Charm against Fever

1. Hence, filled with holy strength let Agni, Soma, and Varuṇa, the Press-stone, and the Altar,
And Grass, and glowing Fuel banish Fever. Let hateful things stay at a distance yonder.

2. And thou thyself who makest all men yellow, consuming them with burning heat like Agni,
Thou, Fever! then be weak and ineffective. Pass hence into the realms below or vanish.

7. Go, Fever, to the Mūjavats, or farther, to the Bāhlīkas.
Seek a lascivious Śūdra girl and seem to shake her through and through.

8. Go hence and eat thy kinsmen the Mahāvṛishas and Mūjavats.
These or those foreign regions we proclaim to Fever for his home.

12. Go Fever, with Consumption, thy brother, and with thy sister, Cough,
And with thy nephew Herpes, go away unto that alien folk.

13. Chase Fever whether cold or hot, brought by the summer or the rains,
Tertian, intermittent, or autumnal, or continual.

14. We to Gandhāris, Mūjavats, to Aṅgas and to Māgadhas
Hand over Fever as it were a servant and a thing of price.

Atharvaveda, V. xxii. 1, 2, 7, 8, 12, 13–14; Griffith, i, pp. 224–5.

TABLES

6. The Chief Charaṇas or Schools with their Brāhmaṇas

Charaṇas	*Brāhmaṇas*
A. Ṛigveda—	
1. The Aitareyins . . .	*Aitareya*
2. The Kaushītakins . .	*Kaushītaki*
B. Sāmaveda—	
1. The Tāṇḍins	*Pañchaviṁśa*
2. The Chhāndogyas . .	[*Chhāndogya*]
3. The Talavakāras . . .	*Talavakāra*
C. Black Yajur—	
1. The Taittirīyins . .	*Taittirīya*
2. The Kāṭhakas	
3. The Maitrayaṇīyas	
C. White Yajur—	
1. The Vājasaneyins . .	*Śatapatha*
D. Atharvaveda—	*Gopatha*

NOTE.—The *Chhāndogya Brāhmaṇa* has not survived, though we have the *Chhāndogya Upanishad.*

7. Relative Age of the Brāhmaṇas

DATES UNKNOWN

External Events	*Indian History*	*Literature*	
Elijah, the Prophet, about 860 B.C.	The Aryans in Kurukshetra	THE BRĀHMAṆAS	
The *Iliad* composed.	Elaboration of the sacrifice	*Pañchaviṁśa*	Gradual Compilation of the *Atharvaveda*
	The Aryans in the Middle Land	*Taittirīya*	
Isaiah, the Prophet, 737–700 B.C.	Writing introduced	*Talavakāra*	
	Rise of the Vānaprasthas	*Kaushītaki*	
		Aitareya	
		Śatapatha	
		Gopatha	

तद्यदेतदिदम्मयोऽदोमय इति
यथाकारी यथाचारी तथा भवति।

CHAPTER IV

PHILOSOPHIC PERIOD

ESSENTIAL HINDUISM

Period ends about 480 B.C.

26. *History.* This period saw the completion of the spread of Aryan influence all over North India, and the still further progress of the organization of the people under the Brāhmans. North India was divided into a large number of different states, of which a few were ruled as republics, but the majority as monarchies. Several of them were of considerable size, and had great military power. The chief of them were undoubtedly Magadha, corresponding roughly to Bihār, and Kosala, corresponding roughly to Oudh. The capitals of these states were now large, prosperous, wealthy cities. Industry, trade, and the simple arts were progressing. A rude coinage, consisting

3. Early Indian Coin

Note.—The text at the top of the page is one of the earliest utterances on KARMA AND REBIRTH :—

'In proportion as a man consists now of this or that, just as he acts, just as he behaves, so will he be born.' *Bṛihadāraṇyaka Upanishad,* IV. iv. 5.

of rectangular pieces of gold, silver, and copper, with a few signs punched on them, was introduced. There were still vast tracts of country under forest, but each of the states contained scenes of busy, happy life; and there was constant communication between all the chief points.

27. *Religion.* During this period the Brāhmans continued their sacrificial work, and also carried on the great task of bringing the aborigines under the influence of Aryan culture. New gods and demigods constantly found their way into the pantheon. The schools of the priests were more important than ever. The city of Taxila in the extreme north-west of the Punjab was the chief centre of learning.

28. Religion as a whole remained much as it was during the previous period. Innumerable sacrifices were still offered, and the old beliefs continued unchanged for most people. But the more intelligent men underwent a revolutionary change.

(*a*) The old hazy pantheistic faith became clear and was grasped more firmly. The whole world was paltry and unreal in comparison with the One which informed it and was its sole Reality. All the ordinary gods were spoken of as mere temporary manifestations of the unchanging and actionless Absolute. Yet the worship of the gods went on unchanged, as the Absolute is unknowable.

(*b*) The problems raised by the very varying fortunes of men and the extraordinary differences in character met with everywhere were solved for the Indian mind by the doctrine of Transmigration and its pendant Karma.

The doctrine of ***Transmigration*** is that souls are emanations of the divine spirit, sparks from the central fire, drops from the ocean of divinity, that each soul is incarnated in a body times without number, that the same soul may be in one life a god, in another a man, in a third an animal or even a plant, and that there can be no rest for the soul nor relief from suffering until it finds release from the necessity of birth and returns to the divine source whence it came.

The word *karma* means literally action, but the doctrine means the inevitable working out of action in new life. The idea is that a man's body, character, capacities and temperament, his birth, wealth and station, and the whole of his experience in life, whether of happiness or of sorrow, together form the just retribution for his deeds, good and bad, done in earlier existences. The expiation works itself out not only in his passive experience (*bhoktṛitvam*), but in his actions also (*kartṛitvam*). Then these new actions form new *karma* which must necessarily be expiated in another existence; so that, as fast as the clock of retribution runs down, it winds itself up again, as Deussen remarks.

(*c*) As it is deeds, good or bad, that form *karma*, and thus lead to rebirth, the idea lies ready to hand that, if by any means a man can cease acting, he may thereby get Release from the necessity of rebirth. Quite naturally and unreflectingly men took action to mean the business of life; so there arose the universal conviction that, if a man wished to reach Release, he must give up the ordinary life of man with all its gains, pleasures and interests and live an actionless existence, turning away from the unreal world and drawing near the one actionless Reality. The ascetic is the only truly religious man, according to this doctrine.

(*d*) It was perhaps the doctrine of the frequent rebirth of souls which suggested the theory of the cyclic destruction and recreation of the world. The idea is that the crude, external, phenomenal world periodically returns to a state of undifferentiated invisibility; souls leave their bodies; and matter and souls remain in undisturbed peace until the moment comes for a new creation. Then matter begins once more to evolve; inorganic things, the vegetable world, animals, men and gods come into being; the process of transmigration begins at the precise point where it stopped when the world disappeared; the castes are re-formed; the *ṛishis* see the Vedas once more; and thus the world comes to be just as it was before.

The period between creation and destruction is called a *kalpa*, the period of repose a *pralaya*. So much is common to all schools of Hindus, and to Buddhists as well. In the subdivision of the *kalpa* a descending series of four ages, corresponding roughly to the golden, silver, bronze, and iron ages of the Classics, is much used, but there are considerable differences in the detailed application of the idea.[1] The Jains drop out the period of repose, and divide time into alternating periods of degeneration and progress. In all schools time has neither beginning nor end.

(*e*) The Brāhman was everywhere accepted as the divine teacher and sacrificer; his Veda was the one Revelation; and Caste was the heaven-sent system for the social organization of the people.

(*f*) This then is essential Hinduism:—

A. *The Theory of God and the world*, consisting of—
   (1) The one impersonal Reality and the unreal phenomenal world, which undergoes cyclic change. All minor gods are gathered under the pantheistic All.
   (2) Transmigration and Karma the explanation of the world.
   (3) Release from Transmigration and union with the one Reality, the object of all serious men.

B. *The organizing conception*, consisting of—
   (1) The divine priest.
   (2) The inspired Veda.
   (3) Caste.

[1] See p. 46.

(*g*) By the time that this new conception of the world had taken distinct form, it had become the custom to send every boy belonging to the Brāhman, Kshatriya, and Vaiśya castes to a Brahmanical school to receive an education. A ceremony of initiation introduced the lad to this religious training. A Brāhman priest muttered sacred texts over him and put the sacred thread on his shoulder; and immediately thereafter his education began. It was a birth into a new life. Hence these three castes are known as twice-born. The fact that every man of these castes spent several years under Brāhman discipline and teaching explains in some degree the extraordinary influence of the priestly class. No one but a Brāhman was allowed to teach. Teaching, sacrificing, and receiving gifts were the three functions which belonged to them by virtue of their birth. This universal education of the boys of the three twice-born castes, coupled with the absolute exclusion of every other one from this, the one avenue to culture and knowledge then open in India, helps to explain the great predominance of these castes throughout India. No arrangement was made for giving girls an education; marriage took the place of initiation in their case.

(*h*) By the end of our period we have trustworthy evidence to prove that two of the most characteristic Hindu customs were regarded as right, namely, the use of idols in worship and child-marriage. The Hindu law enjoined that a girl should be married before she reached the age of puberty, and this necessarily led to child-marriage. We may also note that by this time only the childless widow was allowed to re-marry.

29. This brief outline of Essential Hinduism is sufficient to show us what an overturning change the Indian mind had experienced. The steadily-growing culture of the Brāhmans and the wider experience of men and things which they were daily acquiring as they went on with the work of reducing the whole population of India under their own religious sway had brought them to this new and far-reaching system of thought. Under the wide dome of this universal pantheism they were able to gather all the aboriginal worships of the land and by tactful arrangements to give them a certain distinct unity. The common people continued their worship practically unchanged: only Brāhman teachers taught Transmigration everywhere, and spoke of the great God behind all gods. How different all this is from the beliefs of the *Ṛigveda*!

This radical system has been taught wherever Hinduism has gone; it lies behind all the philosophies and is implied in the asceticism, the laws, the worship, and the life of the people.

NOTE.—The text below is the law of CHILD-MARRIAGE in the earliest Hindu Law-book: 'A girl should be given in marriage before puberty.' Gautama, *Dharmasūtra*, xviii. 21.

प्रदानं प्राग्रृतोः ॥

ILLUSTRATIVE READINGS

5. The One Reality

Who is he whom we meditate on as the self? What is that self? That by which one sees, by which one hears, by which one smells scents, by which one forms speech, by which one discriminates sweet and sour? That which is the heart and the mind, perception, injunction, understanding, knowledge, wisdom, vision, firmness, thinking, considering, helping, memory, resolution, will, breath, love, and desire? All these are only names of knowledge. That (self) is *brahman*, Indra, Prajāpati, all the gods, the five great elements, earth, air, ether, water, lights, all these and those which are mixed with small as it were, seeds of various kinds, born of eggs, born from the womb, born from heat, born from germs, horses, cows, men, elephants, and all that breathes, whether it walks or flies, and what is immovable. All that is guided by knowledge, it rests on knowledge. The world is guided by knowledge. Knowledge is its foundation. Knowledge is *brahman*. He by his knowing self, having left this world and having obtained all delights in the world of heaven, became immortal.

Aitareya Āraṇyaka, ii. 6. From Keith's text and translation in *Anecdota Oxoniensia*.

6. Excommunication

NOTE.—This passage has been selected for reading because it sets forth so clearly a number of the elements of the Hindu system. Here we have the sanctity of the Veda, the privileges of Brāhmans, the restrictions of caste, the sacred cord, the lock of hair on the crown of the head, and excommunication carried out by the performance of the funeral ceremony and *interdictio aquā*, an old Aryan custom. The law here stated as applicable to a Brāhman father who has to be excommunicated by his own son is of course all the more applicable to caste-breakers of lower degree. When a Hindu becomes a Christian by baptism, this law comes into operation, because he 'dwells with men of the lowest castes'.

Let him cast off a father who assassinates a king, who sacrifices for Śūdras, who sacrifices for his own sake, accepting money from Śūdras, who divulges the Veda to persons not authorized to study it, who kills a learned Brāhman, who dwells with men of the lowest castes, or cohabits with a female of one of the lowest castes. Having assembled the sinner's spiritual Gurus and the relatives by marriage, the sons and other kinsmen shall perform for him all the funeral rites, the first of which is the libation of water, and afterwards they shall overturn his water-vessel in the following manner; a slave or a hired servant shall fetch an impure vessel from a dust-heap, fill it with water taken from the pot of a female slave and, his face turned towards the south, upset it with his foot, pronouncing the sinner's name and saying: 'I deprive N. N. of water.' All the kinsmen shall touch the slave, passing their sacrificial cords over the right shoulder and under the left arm, and untying the locks on their heads. The spiritual Gurus and the relatives by marriage shall look on.

Gautama, *Dharmasūtra*, xx. 1–6 (for this book see below, p. 73), *S. B. E.*, vol. ii, pp. 277–8.

TABLES

8. The Ages of the World

There is some reason for thinking that at first the following was the whole scheme of the *Kalpa* :—

Kṛita yuga
Tretā yuga
Dvāpara yuga
Kali yuga
} = *Kalpa*

The names are taken from the game of dice, *Kṛita*, 'the four,' designating the Golden Age, when virtue is four-square ; *Tretā*, 'the three,' designating the Silver Age, when one-fourth part of virtue has been lost ; *Dvāpara*, 'the two,' when one-half of virtue has disappeared ; and *Kali*, 'the one,' when only one-fourth part of good remains. *Yuga* is the Sanskrit word for 'age'.

But the scheme was much elaborated by the various schools ; and the doctrine finally adopted by orthodox Hinduism is that these four ages make one *Mahāyuga* or Great Age, and that it takes 1,000 *Mahāyugas* to complete a *Kalpa*.

The number of dice spots was applied also to the length of the ages as under :—

Dawn	400	= *Kṛita yuga*	= *Mahāyuga*
Day	4,000		
Twilight	400		
Dawn	300	= *Tretā yuga*	
Day	3,000		
Twilight	300		
Dawn	200	= *Dvāpara yuga*	
Day	2,000		
Twilight	200		
Dawn	100	= *Kali yuga*	
Day	1,000		
Twilight	100		

This elaborate scheme arose much later than the philosophic period.

असतो मा सद्गमय
तमसो मा ज्योतिर्गमय
मृत्योर्माऽमृतं गमय ॥

CHAPTER V

PHILOSOPHIC PERIOD CONTINUED

THE UPANISHADS, BUDDHISM AND JAINISM

Period ends about 480 B.C.

30. A time came when there arose a great passion among thinking men in North India to win Release, and many theories as to the true path to Emancipation were proclaimed. Most of the leaders declared that Release was the fruit of knowledge, but others laid stress on sacrifice or Vedic study, and many declared that the true means was *tapas*, austerity. So, many went out to the old hermitages and sought by indescribable self-torture to reach the end of birth and sorrow.

31. But the more serious men went farther. They regarded the whole phenomenal world as inherently antagonistic to the spiritual life. They therefore decided to go much

NOTE.—The text at the top of the page is AN ANCIENT PRAYER from the oldest Upanishad:—

From the unreal lead me to the real!
From darkness lead me to light!
From death lead me to immortality!

Bṛihadāraṇyaka Upanishad, I. iii. 28.

farther than the hermits: they gave up the worship of the gods, ancestor-worship and all family connexions, and became homeless beggars. They might seek Release either by *tapas*, or by knowledge, or by a combination of the two; but in any case they abandoned all connexion with the life of men. This new type of ascetic was called *parivrājaka*, wanderer; *bhikshu*, beggar; *sannyāsī*, renouncer.

32. The attempt to reach Release by means of true knowledge led to momentous results. Many theories of the constitution of the world were formed and taught; but the most important of all is the doctrine of the Upanishads. The ordinary name for the World-soul was *Brahman*, a neuter noun which expresses the common thought of the time, that the World-soul is an impersonal essence present in all things. There were many speculations as to its nature; until some wise thinker called Brahman the *ātman*, or Self of the universe. Then, as the soul of the universe was *ātman*, and the soul of the individual was *ātman*, the conclusion was soon drawn that the two were identical. The great affirmation was made, 'My self is the infinite Self'; 'the soul of the universe, whole and undivided, dwells in me.' Thus self-knowledge is knowledge of God; and, as knowledge of God leads to Release, the man who realizes the identity of his soul with the World-soul is thereby set free from the cycle of births and deaths; he will not be born again. The great phrases used are, 'Thou art That,' 'I am Brahman,' and 'I am He.' This is the Vedānta philosophy in its earliest form.

The conception of Brahman-Ātman in the Upanishads is a great lightning-flash of truth, and it is placed before us in many a noble passage: Brahman is Consciousness: Brahman is the Reality of everything; Brahman is joy; Brahman is incomprehensible; by the command of Brahman all things are done. The phrase, *sachchidānanda Brahma*, 'Brahman is reality, intelligence, and bliss,' is a very late one, not found in this period at all, but it sums up Upanishad thought with great accuracy.

But there is one fatal omission in this conception. Brahman is not conceived as holy: we are nowhere told that Brahman is righteousness. The fact is that the theory of the Ātman is simply a very lofty philosophic presentation of the ancient pagan conception of God. Consequently, the Vedānta philosophy has never been to India what the teaching of the prophets was to Israel. Hinduism remains from first to last crippled, because the idea of God was never moralized.

33. The philosophy of the Ātman sketched above was by no means the only philosophic system put forward as the way to Release. Numerous philosophic leaders stand out dimly in the pale historic light, each with his own specialized doctrine and his following of monks. In an old Buddhist book there is a catalogue of sixty-two different theories of the universe taught at this time in North India. All these system-builders had a great deal in common. Transmigration was accepted as an axiom, and also the beliefs, that earthly things had to be given up if Release was to be won, and that knowledge was the right means of Release. Hence the search for knowledge and the wandering monkish life were universal among philosophers. Women also adopted the wandering life; so that each school had nuns as well as monks.

34. It seems to be certain that the Sāṅkhya system as well as the Vedānta was sketched at this early date, but no treatise of the school belonging to this period survives. Among the numerous teachers of the time two stand out above all others, Mahāvīra, the Jain leader, and Gautama, the founder of Buddhism. They were contemporaries, Mahāvīra the older of the two. Their exact dates are not known as

yet, but it seems clear that Gautama's death occurred within a few years of 480 B.C., the date which closes our period.

35. Jainism was originally merely a specialization and intensification of the old ascetic discipline under the influence of an extreme reverence for life and of a dogmatic belief that not only men, animals, and plants, but the smallest particles of earth, fire, water, and wind are endowed with living souls. Consequently, a very large part of the Jain monk's attention was directed to using the extremest care not to injure any living thing. So eager were the Jains to part with the world to the uttermost that many of their monks wore not a scrap of clothing. Twelve years of most severe asceticism were necessary for salvation. After that, if a monk did not wish to live longer, he was recommended to starve himself to death.

36. Buddhism, on the other hand, while it recommended a mild asceticism, condemned self-torture, and found salvation in *knowledge* and *right living*. The knowledge which Buddha taught was summed up by him in three propositions, known as 'the three characteristics of being', namely :—

All its constituents are transitory;
All its constituents are misery;
All its constituents are lacking in an ego.

If a man realize that all things are fleeting, that life is sorrow, and that he has no soul to save, he will thereby be set free from the chains of the world, and will experience the *nirvāṇa* (i.e. extinction) of lust, hatred, and ignorance. Having reached freedom, he will live his life according to the noble laws of Buddha. Being thus a conqueror over the world, he will at death enter final *nirvāṇa*; he will not be born again.

Buddhism, Jainism, and the Sāṅkhya system fail to teach the existence of the living eternal only God, but they recognize all the godlings of the Hindu system, giving them a very humble place.

37. Philosophic leaders in those days received numerous honorific titles from their followers, *buddha* (enlightened), *jina* (conqueror), *tīrthakara* (ford-maker, i.e. religious leader), &c. Gautama finally became known as the Buddha, Mahāvīra as the Jina (whence the word Jain).

38. Both of these leaders also formed an outer circle of lay followers, who were not required to practise the asceticism of the monks, but obeyed easy regulations.

39. *Literature, &c.* The Brāhmans, perceiving the power of the philosophy of the Ātman, were not slow to adopt it and to introduce it into their schools. There it was taught as a special discipline preparatory to the life of the *parivrājaka*, while ordinary Brāhman pupils took it as an extra subject at the close of the regular priestly course. As this knowledge was regarded as the final aim of all Veda study, it was called *Vedānta*, i.e. Veda-end.

Gradually the allegorical teaching given as a preparation for the hermit life, and the philosophic instruction intended for the wandering life, took definite shape and were handed down orally from teacher to pupil in fixed language, each school having its own sacred deposit. The former was called *āraṇyaka*, or 'forest teaching', as we have seen; the latter *upanishad*, probably in the sense of 'secret doctrine'. Thus were formed the wonderful treatises which we now know as the Āraṇyakas and the Upanishads. It is to be noted that the two types of teaching frequently overlap in one document. To this early period belong only the first great group of prose treatises, written in the style of the Brāhmaṇas, viz. the four Āraṇyakas and the *Bṛihadāraṇyaka*, *Chhāndogya*, *Taittirīya*, *Aitareya*, *Kaushītaki*, and *Kena* Upanishads. These have been used devotionally all through the centuries by a small but select company of intellectual and spiritual men.

40. During this period the theory that the Brāhmaṇas

with their appendices, the Āraṇyakas and the Upanishads, are Revelation, *śruti*, in precisely the same sense as the Vedas themselves, took shape and found acceptance. Indeed it became customary to use the word Veda to cover all this prose literature as well as the hymns; so that one has constantly to ask whether the word is used in the wide or the narrow sense. The theory was that no hymn or Brāhmaṇa had a human author, but that they were eternal, and that they had been 'seen' by the *ṛishis*, i.e. 'seers'. Through this idea the limits of the canon were fixed. All that is *śruti* is included; all that is not *śruti* is excluded. The Veda was held to be so sacred that to reveal any portion of it to any one other than a member of the three highest castes was regarded as a heinous sin (see p. 45). There is a vast amount of sacred literature besides this, but it is only *smṛiti*, 'recollection,' that is Tradition. It has only a limited authority.

41. Towards the end of this period the *Rāmāyaṇa* in its earliest form, which consisted of only five books (ii–vi), was composed by Vālmīki, in the Kingdom of Kosala. In this work Rāma is a purely human hero.

NOTE.—The text below expresses THE JOY OF KNOWING BRAHMAN:—

'He who knows Brahman as Reality, Knowledge, Eternal, he obtains all desires.' *Taittirīya Upanishad*, II. i. 1.

सत्यं ज्ञानमनन्तं ब्रह्म यो वेद
सोऽश्नुते सर्वान् कामान् ॥

ILLUSTRATIVE READINGS

7. The Vānaprastha and the Āśrama

When Rāma, valiant hero, stood
In the vast shade of Daṇḍak wood,
His eyes on every side he bent
And saw a hermit settlement,
Where coats of bark were hung around,
And holy grass bestrewed the ground.
Bright with Brāhmanic lustre glowed
That circle where the saints abode:
Like the hot sun in heaven it shone,
Too dazzling to be looked upon.
Wild creatures found a refuge where
The court, well-swept, was bright and fair,
And countless birds and roedeer made
Their dwelling in the friendly shade.
Beneath the boughs of well-loved trees
Oft danced the gay Apsarases.
Around was many an ample shed
Wherein the holy fire was fed;
With sacred grass and skins of deer,
Ladles and sacrificial gear,
And roots and fruit, and wood to burn,
And many a brimming water-urn.
There, clad in coats of bark and hide—
Their food by roots and fruit supplied—
Dwelt many an old and reverend sire
Bright as the sun or Lord of Fire,
All with each worldly sense subdued,
A pure and saintly multitude.

Vālmīki, *Rāmāyaṇa*, Book III, Canto i; Griffith, p. 228.

8. The Horse of the Aśvamedha

A Meditation for the Vānaprastha

Verily the dawn is the head of the horse which is fit for sacrifice, the sun its eye, the wind its breath, the mouth the Vaiśvānara fire, the year the body of the sacrificial horse. Heaven is the back, the sky the belly, the earth the chest, the quarters the two sides, the intermediate quarters the ribs, the members the seasons, the joints the months and half months, the feet days and nights, the bones the stars, the flesh the clouds. The half-digested food is the sand, the rivers the bowels, the liver and the lungs the mountains, the hairs the herbs and trees. As the sun rises, it is the forepart, as it sets, the hindpart of the horse. When the horse shakes itself, then it lightens; when it kicks, it thunders; when it makes water, it rains; voice is its voice.

Verily Day arose after the horse as the golden vessel, called Mahimān, which at the sacrifice is placed before the horse. Its place is in the Eastern sea. The Night arose after the horse as the silver vessel, called Mahimān, which at the sacrifice is placed behind the horse. Its place is in the Western sea. Verily these two vessels arose to be on each side of the horse.

As a racer he carried the Devas, as a stallion the Gandharvas, as a runner the Asuras, as a horse men. The sea is its kin, the sea is its birthplace.

Bṛihadāraṇyaka Upanishad, i. 1; *S. B. E.* xv. 73-4.

9. The Identity of the Human and the Divine Self

'Place this salt in water, and then wait on me in the morning.'

The son did as he was commanded.

The father said to him: 'Bring me the salt, which you placed in the water last night.'

The son, having looked for it, found it not, for, of course, it was melted.

The father said: 'Taste it from the surface of the water. How is it?'

The son replied: 'It is salt.'

'Taste it from the middle. How is it?'

The son replied: 'It is salt.'

'Taste it from the bottom. How is it?'

The son replied: 'It is salt.'

The father said: 'Throw it away and then wait on me.'

He did so; but salt exists for ever.

Then the father said: 'Here also, in this body, forsooth, you do not perceive the True, my son; but there indeed it is. That which is the subtle essence, in it all that exists has its self. That is the True. That is the Self, and thou, O Śvetaketu, art That.'

Chhāndogya Upanishad, vi. 13; *S.B.E.* i. 104–5.

TABLES

9. The Relative Age of the Early Upanishads

PERIOD ENDS ABOUT 480 B. C.

Events outside India	*History*	*Religion*	*Literature*
Zoroaster, 66c–583 B.C. The *Avesta*	All North India under Aryan influence	Transmigration and Karma accepted	The early prose Upanishads
Jeremiah, 627–580 B.C.	Rise of great cities		1. *Bṛihadāraṇyaka*
		Taxila a seat of learning	
	Coinage appears		2. *Chhāndogya*
		Idols in Hinduism	3. *Taittirīya*
Pythagoras, died about 510 B.C.	Gradual Conquest of the South		4. *Aitareya*
Athens a republic, 510 B.C. Rome a republic, 509 B.C.		Rise of Jainism Rise of Buddhism	5. *Kaushītaki*
			6. *Kena*
		Death of Mahāvīra	
Confucius the Chinese sage, 551–479 B.C.	500 Darius conquers the Punjab	Death of Gautama about 480 B.C.	*The Rāmāyaṇa, II–VI*

10. Śruti, the Hindu Canon

NOTE.—For the *Mahānārāyaṇa* and the other Upanishads which are not mentioned in section 39, see section 51 and p. 73. Many later Upanishads, not included in this table, are recognized as *śruti* also; but they have no definite place in any Vedic school, but are loosely attached to the *Atharvaveda.*

Veda	*Brāhmaṇa* For the Priest	*Āraṇyaka* For the Hermit	*Upanishad* For the Wanderer
Ṛik	1. *Aitareya* 2. *Kaushītaki*	1. *Aitareya* 2. *Kaushītaki*	1. *Aitareya* 2. *Kaushītaki*
Sāman	1. *Pañcha-viṁśa* 2. [*Chhāndo-gya*] 3. *Talavakāra*		2. *Chhāndogya* 3. *Kena*
Black Yajus	1. *Taittirīya* 2. 3.	1. *Taittirīya*	1. *Taittirīya* *Mahānārāyaṇa* 2. *Kāṭhaka* 3. *Maitrāyaṇīya* *Śvetāśvatara*
White Yajus	1. *Śatapatha*	1. *Bṛihat*	1. *Bṛihadāraṇyaka* *Īśā*
Atharvan	*Gopatha*		*Muṇḍaka* *Praśna* *Māṇḍūkya*

BUDDHAṀ ŚARAṆAṀ GACCHĀMI
DHAMMAṀ ŚARAṆAṀ GACCHĀMI
SAṄGHAṀ ŚARAṆAṀ GACCHĀMI

CHAPTER VI

SCHOLASTIC PERIOD

SŪTRAS AND SUTTAS

480 B.C. to 184 B.C.

42. *History.* The greatest fact to be realized with regard to the history of this period is the gradual Aryanizing of South India. We have no detailed account of how it was carried out. Doubtless the chief work was done by Brāhman priests, who went all over the south country as missionaries of the faith and civilization of their people, but Aryan warriors also won themselves kingdoms in the south.

43. Darius conquered the basin of the Indus and a part of the Punjab about 500 B.C., but we do not know how long Persian rule lasted there. Apart from this, North India remained practically as it was before until 321 B.C. The literature speaks of the existence of sixteen leading powers in North India in these centuries. The brilliant invasion of the Punjab by Alexander the Great in 326 B.C.

NOTE.—The text at the top of the page is the FORMULA OF ENTRANCE INTO BUDDHISM, 'I take refuge in the Buddha; I take refuge in the Doctrine; I take refuge in the Order.' The language is Pāli.

did not disturb appreciably the other parts of India; and very soon after his death in 323 B.C. a revolt destroyed the Greek power in the Punjab.

44. But the young adventurer who overthrew the Greeks in the Punjab soon brought the whole of the northern half of India under his rule, and thus founded the first empire ever known in India (321 B.C.). His name was Chandragupta, and *Pāṭaliputra*, i. e. Patna, the capital of Magadha, was his capital. His grandson, Aśoka (272–231 B.C.), ruled a large part of South India also. Under this man, a ruler of the highest capacity and character, civilization made great strides. Stone architecture and sculpture made their appearance in India during his reign, and from his time onwards inscriptions are common. His descendants, however, proved unfit for imperial power; and the empire gradually weakened and finally broke up in 184 B.C. After Alexander the coinage of India became artistic under the influence of the mints of Greece, Bactria, and Persia.

4. HINDU IDOLATRY

The earliest surviving representations of Hindu idols occur in Buddhist sculpture. This is the goddess Śrī from the Bharhut Stūpa, now in Calcutta Museum (Cunningham, xxvi). See below, p. 62.

45. *Religion.* During this period Hinduism with its Veda and caste-system, its priests and regulated worship, completed the conquest of the peninsula. From this time onwards the Brāhmans are everywhere recognized as divine representatives of the gods. But, although they became supreme wherever they went, and brought the better part of the population under their care, there were large sections of the people everywhere whom they considered

too low and degraded to receive their ministrations. The descendants of these groups are found to this day in all parts of the country. In the south a very large proportion of the population was held to be so unclean as to be beyond the pale of Brāhman service; and the millions of their descendants still remain outside (see Chapter XV).

5. A HINDU TEMPLE IN BUDDHIST SCULPTURE

From the Sāñchī Stūpa of second century B.C. (Maisey, xiii.). See fig. 6. The divinity is a five-headed snake, or Nāga, which is visible within the shrine. In front stands a fire-altar, while a Vānaprastha and his leafy hut may be seen in the right foreground.

This period is scholastic in most of its religious features. Hindu practice became steadily more regular under the unceasing pressure of priestly authority. This is most noteworthy in the realm of social life; at the beginning of the period there was still a considerable amount of caste laxity throughout Northern India, but by the close a great advance had taken place. The whole system had hardened and was very much what it has been for centuries. A large number of the secondary castes were already in existence. One of the chief characteristics of the priesthood at this time was the desire to express everything with great exactness in well-arranged manuals, each devoted to a single subject. This scholastic tendency comes out very distinctly in Buddhist literature also; everything is classified, arranged in groups, numbered and labelled. There are four Noble Truths; the Noble Path is eight-fold; there are twelve steps in the theory of Dependent Origination, the Buddhist theory of how living beings come into existence. The same is true of Jainism.

6. North Gate of the Sāñchī Stūpa.

This noble monument stands at Sāñchī in the Bhopāl State. The huge mound of the stūpa is visible behind the gate, but the ornament on the top is gone. Portions of the stone rail are visible on each side of the gate. There are three other gates. (Photograph by Johnston & Hoffmann.)

Images and temples rose during this period to the place which they have ever since held in Hindu life. The traditional appearance of the various gods, with their dress, weapons, and ornaments, became definitely fixed; while the plan of the temple court was modelled on the arrangements of the ground for the ancient sacrifices.

46. When Gautama the Buddha died, his relics, divided into seven portions, were laid in seven stūpas erected for them; and the great teachers who followed him were similarly honoured. Nor was that all. Buddhists soon began to believe that the truth had been taught by a long

7. BUDDHIST WORSHIP

Men and angels adoring a stūpa. This is a relief from the rail of the Bharhut Stūpa of the second century B.C., now in Calcutta Museum. Cunningham, *Stūpa of Bharhut*, xxxi.

succession of Buddhas before Gautama, and that in the next age another, named Maitreya, would arise. (See p. 97.) All these things stirred feelings of piety and reverence in Buddhist hearts. Crowds of lay believers bowed down before the great stūpas in reverent meditation, adoring the relics and repeating sacred formulas, and walked round the stūpas in solemn religious march. To these observances and to the stated gatherings in the *chaityas*, or assembly halls, we must attribute the beginnings of Buddhist worship.

47. In the ninth year of his reign Aśoka became a Buddhist layman. Later he actually became a monk. He spent a great deal of energy in trying to lead his subjects to the adoption of the moral teaching of Buddhism. For this purpose, he had long edicts cut on rocks in various

8. BUDDHIST WORSHIP

A *chaitya* or Buddhist hall and Buddhists adoring a *dharmachakra*, or wheel of the doctrine, a symbol of Buddha's teaching. A relief from the Bharhut Stūpa. Cunningham, xxxi.

parts of his empire, calling on the people to cultivate filial piety, righteousness, reverence for all religions, and kindness to animals. He erected hospitals for man and beast, and in every way sought the welfare of his subjects. Innumerable religious edifices were erected to his order, chiefly stūpas, chaityas, monasteries, and rock-cut cells for monks. But the most significant act of his reign was the sending out of missionaries to spread Buddhism throughout India and the neighbouring lands. As a result Ceylon became a Buddhist country, and the religion also made great progress beyond the river Indus and upon the Himalayas. It was Aśoka that made Buddhism a world-conquering power.

48. The first beginnings of worship among the Jains appeared in much the same way as they did in Buddhism; but this community was not so successful at this time in securing royal and wealthy patrons as the Buddhists were. Their earliest monuments are two to three centuries later.

Then the Jain community broke in two in A.D. 82. It was a question of clothes that led to the separation. The monks of one section wore no clothing and were, therefore, called *Digambara*, 'clothed-in-atmosphere,' while the monks of the other group wore white robes and were called *Śvetāmbara*, 'clothed-in-white.'

49. *Literature.* Quite early in this period, the earliest form of the great epic, the *Mahābhārata*, appeared. It probably arose in the country between the Ganges and the Jumna. It was then a poem of very moderate length, containing about 8,800 couplets, and was called the *Bhārata*. Kṛishṇa is a purely human hero in it.

50. The teaching of each philosophic leader was handed down orally in his monastic school. It is noteworthy, however, that Sanskrit was used in the Brāhmanic schools, while the Jains and the Buddhists used the vernaculars.

As knowledge grew and the compass and the number of the subjects taught in the Brāhmanical schools went on increasing, the mass of material to be learned by rote became more and more unmanageable. It became impossible for the student to store in his memory everything which he wanted to know, so long as it was presented to him in the extraordinarily prolix manner of the Brāhmaṇas. A new method was therefore invented. All the knowledge which the student had to acquire was expressed in strings of aphorisms of the briefest and most pregnant description. As time went on and the new method developed, it became a conventional system of technical terms like a modern telegraphic code. These tabloids of condensed knowledge were called *sūtras*. Is not this the very climax of scholasticism? These books, if books they can be called when they were not written down, dealt with all the subjects of a priest's education. They were usually summed up under six heads, called the *vedāṅgas*, or members of the body of the Veda. Of the six, Kalpa, ceremonial, is the most important. Under Kalpa there are three groups of *sūtras*, the *Śrauta Sūtras*, which deal with the sacrifices, summarizing the teaching of the Brāhmaṇas, the *Gṛihya Sūtras*, which deal with domestic ceremonies, and the *Dharma Sūtras*, which provide rules of conduct for the various classes of men and the various stages of life. The Brāhmanical schools were now more numerous than ever, many of the earlier schools having split into several branches; and each had its own series of *sūtras*, dealing in turn with all the subjects comprehended under the six *vedāṅgas*. Pāṇini, the great grammarian, wrote in *sūtras*, and his work comes under *vyākaraṇa*, one of the *vedāṅgas* (see p. 76). He was connected with Taxila and flourished about 300 B.C.

The language used in the Brāhmanical schools was gradually polished and brought under phonetic and grammatical rules, while, with the spread of the people all over North India, the ordinary language had necessarily developed into a number of provincial vernaculars. The literary tongue of the schools was called *saṁskṛita*, i.e. polished, while the vernaculars were called *prākṛita*, i.e. natural. Pāṇini's grammar finally fixed the form of Sanskrit. Already in his day it was very distinct from the popular dialects. These latter naturally continued to change, and they have produced the great modern Aryan languages of India, Hindī, Punjābī, Gujarātī, Marāṭhī, Bengali, Oṛiyā, Assamese, and the rest.

51. In certain of the schools at this time some of the best parts of the old Upanishads were versified and strung together, so as to make new Upanishads. (See p. 73.) The brief, pointed, aphoristic character of these poems shows plainly that they were put together with a view to their being easily committed to memory.

52. As we have seen, the Jains and the Buddhists used, not Sanskrit, but the vernaculars in teaching their hearers. Their sermons were called *suttas*, which is the vernacular form of the Sanskrit *sūtras*. These were handed down by word of mouth from teacher to pupil; but during the earliest generations they were considerably changed and expanded.

By the year 200 B.C. the Buddhist *Tripiṭaka*, that is, the triple basket, or canon in three parts, was practically complete. Many of these *suttas* are beautiful as literature, and are filled with a love of righteousness and a mounting passion for spiritual things which give them great distinction. When Buddhism was destroyed in India, this literature perished also, but it has been most faithfully preserved in Ceylon. The language of the *Tripiṭaka* is called *Pāli*. This is not the name of any old Indian vernacular, but merely the Singhalese word for 'text', which has come to be used to designate the language of the text, in contrast with the Singhalese of the commentary. Scholars have not been able to decide as yet which of the old Indian vernaculars, through being used by the monks who won Ceylon to the faith, has been preserved for us in the Pāli text.

Jain teaching was similarly handed down, but reached its permanent form later still.

Many other schools had their traditional *suttas*, but they were necessarily lost when the school died out.

NOTE.—The text below is a mnemonic verse giving the names of THE SIX VEDĀṄGAS:—*śikshā*, pronunciation; *kalpa*, ceremonial; *vyākaraṇa*, grammar; *nirukta*, etymology; *chhandas*, metre; *jyotisha*, astronomy.

शिक्षा कल्पो व्याकरणं
निरुक्तं छन्दो ज्योतिषं ॥

ILLUSTRATIVE READINGS

10. Sūtras

NOTE.—A literal translation of each sūtra is given in italics, and then the meaning follows in roman. For a more condensed example see p. 94.

1. *Now, therefore, the right.*

   Now, therefore, the right of performing sacrificial acts will be laid down here.

2. *Acts fruit-attended.*

   Sacrificial acts are attended by fruits, such as heaven, wealth, &c.

3. *Of all without distinction.*

   One would expect that there must be a right of all living beings without distinction to perform sacrificial acts, as all desire fruits.

4. *But of human beings from the power of undertaking.*

   But the right belongs to human beings only, because they only have the power of undertaking sacrificial acts.

5. *Cripple, ignorant, eunuch, Śūdra except.*

   Cripples, those ignorant of the Veda, eunuchs, Śūdras are to be excepted.

6. *Of Brāhmans, Rājanyas, Vaiśyas, from śruti.*

   The right belongs to Brāhmans, Kshatriyas and Vaiśyas, but not to Śūdras, according to Vedic precept.

7. *A woman also without distinction.*

   A woman also has the right, as there is no distinction between her and her husband.

Kātyāyana, *Śrauta Sūtra*, i. 1–7.

II. A Buddhist Sutta

Thus have I heard.

On a certain occasion The Blessed One was dwelling at Sāvatthi in Jetavana monastery in Anāthapiṇḍika's Park. And there The Blessed One addressed the monks.

'Monks,' said he.

'Lord,' said the monks to The Blessed One in reply.

And The Blessed One spoke as follows:

'I will teach you, O monks, the burden, the bearer of the burden, the taking up of the burden, and the laying down of the burden.

'And what, O monks, is the burden?

'Reply should be made that it is the five attachment-groups. And what are the five? They are: the form-attachment-group, the sensation-attachment-group, the perception-attachment-group, the predisposition-attachment-group, the consciousness-attachment-group. These, O monks, are called the burden.

'And who, O monks, is the bearer of the burden?

'Reply should be made that it is the individual; the venerable So-and-so of such-and-such a family. He, O monks, is called the bearer of the burden.

'And what, O monks, is the taking up of the burden?

'It is desire leading to rebirth, joining itself to pleasure and passion, and finding delight in every existence—desire, namely, for sensual pleasure, desire for permanent existence, desire for transitory existence. This, O monks, is called the taking up of the burden.

'And what, O monks, is the laying down of the burden?

'It is the complete absence of passion, the cessation, giving up, relinquishment, forsaking, and non-adoption of desire. This, O monks, is called the laying down of the burden.'

Saṁyutta-Nikāya, xxii. 22, 1; Warren's *Buddhism in Translations*, p. 159.

12. A Passage from a Verse Upanishad

As the one fire that passed into the world
Has there transformed itself to many forms,
So the one Self within all creatures
Transforms itself to many forms, while outside all.

As the one air that passed into the world
Has there transformed itself to many forms,
So the one Self within all creatures
Transforms itself to many forms, while outside all.

Just as the sun, the whole world's eye,
By visible external foulness ne'er is tainted,
So the one Self within all creatures
By the world's sorrow ne'er is tainted, being outside it.

The one Controller, the Self within all creatures,
Who makes the one form manifold—
Those wise men who behold Him in the self,
They and no others have eternal joy.

He who, Eternal, Conscious, One, fulfils
The longings of the Transient, Conscious, Many—
Those wise men who behold Him in the self,
They and no others have eternal peace.

The truth, that this is That, they feel to be
Bliss indescribable, supreme.
How can I come to know it?
Shines it effulgent, or reflecting light?

There shineth not the sun, nor moon and stars;
These lightnings shine not; how much less this fire!
His lonely shining makes the All resplendent!
'Tis with His glory that this whole world gleams!

Kāṭhaka Upanishad, v. 9–15.

13. Buddhist Teaching in Verse

Do not follow the evil law! Do not live on in thoughtlessness! Do not follow false doctrine! Be not a friend of the world.

Rouse thyself! do not be idle! Follow the law of virtue! The virtuous rests in bliss in this world and in the next.

Follow the law of virtue; do not follow that of sin. The virtuous rests in bliss in this world and in the next.

Look upon the world as you would on a bubble, look upon it as you would on a mirage; the king of death does not see him who thus looks down upon the world.

Come, look at this world, glittering like a royal chariot: the foolish are immersed in it, but the wise do not touch it.

He who formerly was reckless and afterwards became sober, brightens up this world, like the moon when freed from clouds.

He whose evil deeds are covered by good deeds, brightens up this world, like the moon when freed from clouds.

This world is dark, few only can see here; a few only go to heaven, like birds escaped from the net.

The uncharitable do not go to the world of the gods; fools only do not praise liberality; a wise man rejoices in liberality, and through it becomes blessed in the other world.

Better than sovereignty over the earth, better than going to heaven, better than lordship over all worlds, is the reward of Sotāpatti, the first step in holiness.

Dhammapada, 167-174, 177-178; *S.B.E.* x. 47.

14. Sātyaki's Sons slain

Morning with her fiery radiance oped the portals of the day,
Shone once more on Kuru warriors, Pāṇḍav chiefs in dread array!

Bhīma and the gallant Arjun led once more the van of war,
But the proud preceptor Droṇa faced them in his sounding car!

Still with gallant son of Arjun, Lakshman strove with bow and shield,
Vainly strove; his faithful henchman bore him bleeding from the field!

Lakshman, son of proud Duryodhan! Abhimanyu, Arjun's son!
Doomed to die in youth and glory 'neath the same revolving sun!

Sad the day for Vṛishṇi warriors! Brave Sātyaki's sons of might,
'Gainst the cruel Bhūri-śravas strove in unrelenting fight,

Ten brave brothers, pride of Vṛishṇi, fell upon that fatal day,
Slain by mighty Bhūri-śravas, and upon the red field lay!

Mahābhārata, R. C. Dutt's version, p. 109.

TABLES

II. Scholastic Period. 480 to 184 B.C.

Sūtras are the characteristic type of Hindu literature throughout this period. The *Gautama Dharmasūtra*, which is the earliest of the Dharma class, probably dates from the end of the philosophic period, and one or two of the Śrauta class may be as early. In any case, all three classes, Śrauta, Gṛihya and Dharma, continued to be composed throughout the period. They are not set down in this table, because their chronological order is not yet accurately known.

External events	*History*	*Religion*	*Literature*	
	Continued conquest of the South		VERSE UPANISHADS	Earliest form of the *Mahābhārata*
400 Socrates drinks the hemlock, 399 B.C.			*Kāṭhaka*	
Plato, 427–347			*Īśā*	
Aristotle, 384–322				
The AVESTA burned by Alexander	Alexander in the Punjab		*Śvetāśvatara*	Gradual Formation of the Buddhist Pāli Canon, the Tripiṭaka
300				
	Aśoka	Rise of Buddhist architecture Buddhist missionaries sent out by Aśoka	*Muṇḍaka*	
200			*Mahānārāyaṇa*	
184	Fall of Aśokan Empire			

12. Conspectus of the Chief

NOTE.—This table is meant to show at a glance the way in which the Vedic literature grew up, and to which school each great manual belongs. The numbers show the school connexion: thus the great Taittirīya school of the Black Yajur Veda had a full series of manuals, Brāhmaṇa, Āraṇyaka, Upanishad, Śrauta, Gṛihya, and Dharma sūtras. Brackets are used to keep together the branch schools belonging to each ancient *charaṇa*. Where there is uncertainty as to the school to

Śruti			
Veda	*Brāhmaṇa*	*Āraṇyaka*	*Upanishad*
ṚIK	1. *Aitareya* 2. *Kaushītaki*	1. *Aitareya* 2. *Kaushītaki*	1. *Aitareya* 2. *Kaushītaki*
SĀMAN	1. *Pañchaviṁśa* 2. [*Chhāndogya*] 3. *Talavakāra*		2. *Chhāndogya* 3. *Kena*
BLACK YAJUS	1. *Taittirīya* 2. 3.	1. *Taittirīya*	1. *Taittirīya*, *Mahānārāyaṇa* 2. *Kāṭhaka* 3. *Maitrāyaṇīya*, *Śvetāśvatara*
WHITE YAJUS	1. *Śatapatha*	1. *Bṛihat*	1. *Bṛihadāraṇyaka*, *Īśā*
ATHARVAN	*Gopatha*		*Muṇḍaka* *Praśna* *Māṇḍūkya*

Manuals of the Vedic Schools

which a manual belongs, no number is prefixed to the name, as in the case of the *Vasishṭha Dharmasūtra*. One *Dharmasūtra* has been put in brackets: the reason is that no manuscript of it has been found; it is known only by quotation; but it is mentioned, because it is the source whence the *Mānava Dharmaśāstra* (see section 62) sprang. All this literature was taught only by Brāhmans and only to men of the three twice-born castes. Women and men of other castes were not allowed to hear it.

Smṛiti

Śrauta Sūtra	*Gṛihya Sūtra*	*Dharma Sūtra*
1. *Āśvalāyana* 2. *Śāṅkhāyana*	1. *Āśvalāyana* 2. { *Śāṅkhāyana* *Śāmbavya*	*Vasishṭha*
1. { *Maśaka* *Drāhyāyaṇa* *Lāṭyāyana*	1. { *Gobhila* *Khādira*	1. *Gautama*
1. { *Baudhāyana* *Āpastamba* *Hiraṇyakeśin* *Bhāradvāja* 3. *Mānava* 1. *Kātyāyana*	1. { *Baudhāyana* *Āpastamba* *Hiraṇyakeśin* *Bhāradvāja* 2. *Kāṭhaka* 3. *Mānava* 1. *Pāraskara*	1. { *Baudhāyana* *Āpastamba* *Hiraṇyakeśin* [3. *Mānava*]
Vaitāna *Kauśika*	*Kauśika*	

13. Interrelations of Vedic Literature

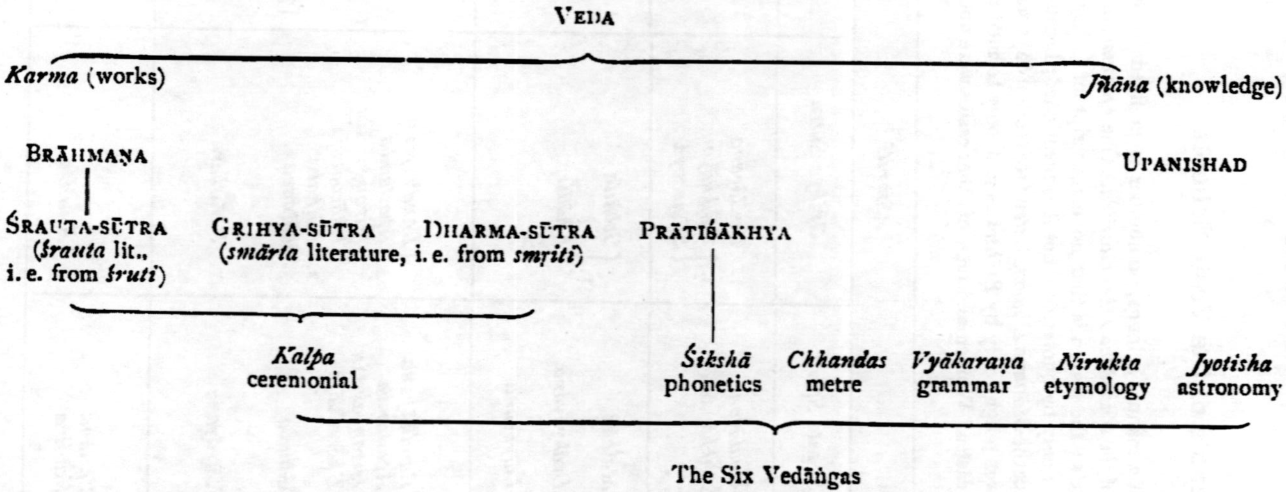

14. The Buddhist Tripiṭaka

1. *The Vinaya Piṭaka:* the Discipline Basket, the rules of the monastic life.[1]

- (a) *Sutta Vibhaṅga.*
- (b) *Khandhakas.*
  - (1) Mahāvagga.
  - (2) Chullavagga.
- (c) *Parivāra.*

2. *The Sutta Piṭaka:* the Sermon Basket, the teaching of the Buddha.

- (a) *Dīgha Nikāya.*
- (b) *Majjhima Nikāya.*
- (c) *Saṁyutta Nikāya.*
- (d) *Aṅguttara Nikāya.*
- (e) *Khuddaka Nikāya.*

3. *The Abhidhamma Piṭaka:* the Exposition Basket, an enlarged and detailed treatment of Buddhist doctrine.

- (a) *Dhamma Saṅgaṇi.*
- (b) *Vibhaṅga.*
- (c) *Kathā Vatthu.*
- (d) *Puggala Paññatti.*
- (e) *Dhātu Kathā.*
- (f) *Yamakas.*
- (g) *Paṭṭhāna.*

[1] This part of the Buddhist canon was kept secret by the monks, and was not revealed even to the Buddhist laity. Most of the monastic orders seem to have refused to divulge their disciplinary rules.

15. The Four Āśramas or Stages of Brāhmanic Life

During the scholastic period, it was recognized that the ideal life for a Brāhman was to spend twelve years as a student, then to marry and beget children, and then to retire to the forest as a hermit, taking his wife with him, if he chose to do so.

At a still later date a fourth stage was added: the Brāhman was recommended, after he had lived as a hermit, to end his days as a houseless *parivrājaka*, thinking only of God.

1. *Brahmachārī*: student.
2. *Gṛihastha*: householder, the ordinary Brāhman priest.
3. *Vānaprastha*: forest-dweller, hermit.
4. *Parivrājaka*: wanderer, houseless monk.

परित्राणाय साधूनां विनाशाय च दुष्कृताम्।
धर्मसंस्थापनार्थाय संभवामि युगे युगे॥

CHAPTER VII

INCARNATION PERIOD

POLITICAL TROUBLES: THE DHARMAŚĀSTRAS

From the Fall of the Aśokan Empire to the Rise of the Guptas, 184 B.C. to A.D. 320

53. *History.* The largest fact in the history of these centuries is the irruption of hordes of invaders from Central Asia across the Indus both in the north and in the south. Necessarily these invasions created great disturbances, and produced considerable mixture in the population of the frontier provinces. The break-up of the Aśokan Empire also led to many revolutions and upheavals. There was thus much violence and frequent political change throughout these centuries in Northern and Central India. We need not here catalogue the many various dynasties which followed each other east, west, north, and south. We need only notice the rise of the one great empire which appeared during our period. This was the kingdom of the Kushāns, a people from Central Asia, their greatest ruler being Kanishka. Peshāwar was their capital; and that city, during the first and second centuries of our era, was the centre of a

NOTE.—The text at the top of the page is A COUPLET ON INCARNATION put into the mouth of Kṛishṇa: 'To save the righteous, to destroy evil-doers, to establish the Law, I come into birth age after age.' *Bhagavadgītā*, iv. 8.

flourishing civilization in which Indian ideas mingled freely with the influence of Persia and of the Roman Empire. These kings would appear to have favoured Hinduism and Zoroastrianism quite as much as Buddhism; yet the latter religion clearly dominated the country round Peshāwar. Architecture flourished, and a famous school of sculpture arose under Greek influence. The art of the kingdom is known as Gandhāran art (see Figs. 9, 11, 14, 16 and pp. 198 and 202). Buddhism found a new base for its operations in Peshāwar; and Sanskrit first came to the front as the common language of India in the Kushān Empire.

9. RELIC-CASKET

Recently discovered in the ruins of Kanishka's stūpa at Peshāwar. The casket is of dark metal and is seven inches high. Contained a rock-crystal reliquary containing bones, said to be Buddha's. On top of casket Buddha and two other figures. Note the haloes. Beneath is Kanishka himself. (From *Journal of Royal Asiatic Society*.)

54. *Religion*. Under Aśoka and his obscure successors Buddhism was greatly favoured. Vast sums of money were spent on Buddhist buildings; and it seems clear from Aśoka's edicts that various laws and regulations were enforced which would please Buddhist monks and would necessarily greatly displease Brāhmans. With the fall of the great empire and the rise of the Śuṅgas to power in Magadha, the tables were turned; for the new dynasty favoured the Brāhmans as much as the old favoured Buddhism. Patañjali, author of the Commentary on Pāṇini's Sūtras and founder of the Yoga philosophy, was the priest of Pushyamitra, the first

Śuṅga king, and refers to his celebration of the Aśvamedha, or horse-sacrifice, which is a public claim to imperial power. The influence and favour of the court led to great literary activity on the part of the priests.

55. The main feature of the religious history of the period as a whole is this, that Hinduism and Buddhism now stand opposed to each other as rivals, and influence each other very greatly in many ways.

10. THE BOAR INCARNATION OF VISHṆU

This relief is at Mahāvellipore. It represents Vishṇu in his boar *avatāra* with his wife Lakshmī. Beneath is a five-hooded Nāga, or divine snake. (Photograph by Wiele & Klein.)

56. One very noteworthy change occurred in Hinduism at this time and, as we shall see, a similar change passed over Buddhism. While at the beginning of the fifth century B.C. Rāma and Kṛishṇa were but human heroes, they were already worshipped in the time of Megasthenes, the Seleucid ambassador at the court of Chandragupta; and by the opening of the second century B.C. they were acknowledged to be incarnations of Vishṇu. In the first and last books of the *Rāmāyaṇa*, which were written in the second century B.C., Rāma is represented as an incarnation of *half* the essence of Vishṇu, and in the additions made to the *Mahābhārata* about the same time Kṛishṇa is regarded as a minor divinity and in some sense as an incarnation of Vishṇu. (See section 63.)

During the next three centuries this rich warm worship of incarnate divinities became entwined with the philosophy of the Ātman, and first Kṛishṇa and then Rāma rose to the lofty position of incarnations of the Supreme. Kṛishṇa occurs in this guise in the latest parts of the *Mahābhārata*, dating perhaps from the second century A.D., and also in the *Bhagavadgītā*. (See sections 63 and 64.)

Certain of the old myths of the Vedas and Brāhmaṇas were transformed into incarnations of Vishṇu, and others were created. The series of semi-animal and other incarnations (*avatāras* is the Hindu word) which are supposed to have preceded Rāma and Kṛishṇa was thus formed. This

11. HINDU IDOLATRY

A coin of Kadphises II, the Kushān king who preceded Kanishka. The reverse gives us Śiva with his bull and his trident. Time, first century A.D. (V. Smith, *Early History of India.*)

long line of Vishṇuite incarnations is parallel to the long list of mythical Buddhas which grew up in the Buddhist Church and the similar list of mythical Tīrthakaras which took form in Jainism at this time. (See p. 97.) These new forms of faith, so well calculated to stir emotion and to provoke enthusiastic worship, naturally led to a great growth of Vishṇuism. The leading school of Vishṇuites were called Bhāgavatas, i.e. worshippers of the Bhagavān, the Adorable Lord. Unlike the teachers of the Vedānta, who held that only the three highest castes could reach Release, because they alone were allowed to read the Upanishads, the Bhāgavatas offered salvation to all.

But the cult of Śiva did not lag behind. The sacred bull became his companion; the trident was connected with him; the phallic symbol, the *liṅga*, was adopted for his worship; and he was represented as the typical ascetic. Vishṇu in

12. BUDDHIST CHAITYA

Excavated in the solid rock at Kārle, near Poona. In these assembly-halls a small stūpa, introduced to inspire meditation, led to real worship. The resemblance to a Christian church is very striking. Here we have the nave with its apse, and the stūpa taking the place of the altar. There are aisles behind the fine Persian pillars. Date, first century B.C. (Photograph by Clifton & Co., Bombay.)

his incarnations, and Śiva with these fresh attractions, now stand side by side with Brahmā. (See p. 99.) The words *Śaivas* and *Vaishṇavas* are used for the followers of these gods.

57. It was during this period that the six systems of philosophy which are recognized as orthodox by Hindus were worked out in detail. Each took shape in its own school, gradually developed and expounded by a succession of teachers. They expressed the system in sūtras in the briefest possible way, and explained the sūtras by means of a commentary. Many of these ancient sūtra manuals have perished, but several survive, of which the greatest is the manual of the Vedānta school, the *Vedānta-sūtras* of Bādarāyaṇa. Table 17 gives the main facts about these systems.

13. IMAGE OF BUDDHA
Beside the *bodhi* tree at Anurādhapura, Ceylon. (From a postcard.)

58. Buddhism, which originally was an agnostic philosophy attempting to do the work of a religion, early developed the beginnings of a worship, as we have already seen. During the first half of this period another step was taken. Images of Buddha, his chief disciples, the previous Buddhas and Maitreya, the coming Buddha, were set up at the stūpas, in pagodas and chaityas. Though the original purpose was merely to stimulate meditation, and though the monks usually kept themselves to that, the necessary result was that the common people worshipped the images. Offerings of flowers and fruit were presented to them; incense and tapers were burned before them; and prayers were uttered with humble adoration and fervent praise. Thus far early Buddhism went; and we have this form still preserved for us practically unaltered in Burma and Ceylon.

59. But the kingdom of the Kushāns was the scene of a still more significant change. Buddhism up to this time had contained many philosophic schools, but there had been no schism. In the great intellectual activity of the Kushān Empire, however, there came a development of worship and theology which split the Buddhist world in two. The new system, which finally received the name Mahāyāna (great path) in contrast with the old, which was called Hīnayāna (humble path), soon became very popular. In it we meet the new doctrine, borrowed from Hinduism, that behind all things there is the universal soul of which the Buddhas are but manifestations. Under the old system the great ideal for the monk was to become an *arhat*, that is a perfect man, destined at death to pass into *nirvāṇa*; but the ideal of the Mahāyāna was the *Bodhisattva*, a being who might become a Buddha and enter *nirvāṇa* but denies himself that luxury, that he may remain in the heavenly regions a gracious and powerful divinity ready to help those that appeal to him. But the chief difference lies in this, that the Hīnayāna saved the few, while the Mahāyāna offered Release to the many.

14. BODHISATTVA FROM YUSUFZAI
V. Smith, *Indian Art*, fig. 63.

The leaders of the Mahāyāna frankly treated the Buddhas and the Bodhisattvas as gods, and set up a most elaborate system of worship. In front of the images in the chaitya an altar was erected on which offerings were made. The chaitya thus became a temple and the monk a priest. Prayers were composed, and a special liturgy for each great divinity. Each accessory that was likely to make the worship attractive and pleasing to the people was added—richly decorated altars, paintings, gorgeous robes, music, processions, banners, incense, &c. Thus Buddhism, originally an agnostic philosophy, became one of the polytheisms and idolatries of the world. The list of the Buddhas is given on p. 97.

15. Mahāyāna Worship
Small stūpa with image of Buddha carved on it, at Kenheri, near Bombay. (Photograph kindly favoured by Mr. Frank Anderson, Bombay.)

Buddha himself was transformed into a Saviour god, incarnate for the good of men, as we may see from the *Lalita Vistara*, the *Saddharma Puṇḍarīka*, and other works of the first and second centuries A. D. Thus the same spirit that worked in Hinduism worked in Buddhism. The *Gītā* and the *Saddharma Puṇḍarīka* are parallel compositions.

60. The most interesting of all the new divinities of this date is Amitābha, who is described in the *Amitāyus Sūtra* and a number of other books written in North India during our period. This Buddha is said to live now in a glorious paradise in the West; but, when he was still a Bodhisattva, he vowed that he would never accept *nirvāṇa* until some means were provided whereby all mankind would be able to receive salvation through faith in him. The worship of this imaginary god cannot now be traced in the history of ancient India, except in sculpture; but it was carried into China, where he is still worshipped, and into Japan, where the two most vigorous sects of our time are worshippers of Amida, the Japanese corruption of Amitābha.

16. MAHĀYĀNA WORSHIP

A piece of devotional sculpture from the Kushān Empire, found at Sahri Bahlol in N. W. F. Province. Gautama Buddha is in the centre, Avalokiteśvara on the left, Maitreya on the right. These two are Bodhisattvas. (From *Archaeological Survey*, 1906-7, p. 114.)

61. *Literature, &c.* During the first half of this period the scholars of India began to use the art of writing for their books. The Buddhist Tripiṭaka was reduced to writing in Ceylon about 85 B.C., and we may be certain that about the same time, or earlier, a similar process was carried out in India, among Hindus as well as Buddhists.

62. We found in each Brāhmanical school the subject of ***dharma***, or the right behaviour of the Hindu in every station of life, dealt with in a Dharmasūtra. In this new period these rules of conduct were gradually rewritten in a popular versified form to be used by the Hindu householder outside the schools. The poems thus produced are known as the

Dharmaśāstras. The greatest of all these law-books is the *Mānava Dharmaśāstra*, or law-book of Manu, which is believed to have been founded on the *Mānava Dharma-sūtra*. Its growth seems to cover several centuries. It had reached its present shape by A. D. 200. One of the momentous changes in Hindu life which this fresh code enables

17. MAHĀYĀNA WORSHIP.

This is a bronze image of Vairochana, a Buddha of light, at Nara, in Japan. It is 53½ feet in height. These gigantic images were common in India. (From a postcard.)

us to realize is this, that all widows, even virgin child-widows, were by this time forbidden to remarry.

63. It seems most likely that the first and the last books of the *Rāmāyaṇa* were added about the beginning of our period. Here Rāma is represented as an incarnation of *half* the essence of Vishṇu and the *Rāmāyaṇa* thereby becomes a Vishṇuite work. About the same time large additions were

made to the *Mahābhārata*, which made it an epic of 24,000 ślokas. In the new matter Kṛishṇa is a demi-god. The re-creation and re-publication of these great works, which glorify Hindu kings and Hindu life and worship, was almost certainly carried out under the patronage of the Śuṅgas.

About four centuries later (*c.* A. D. 200) vast quantities of new matter were introduced into the *Mahābhārata*, transforming the epic into a didactic library. Among the additions was the *Bhagavadgītā*. Here and elsewhere in the new matter Kṛishṇa is represented as the Ātman incarnate.

The two epics are the earliest popular literature of India. They sprang from the heart of the people; and though the *Rāmāyaṇa* was edited for a sectarian purpose, and the *Mahābhārata* has been perverted by the Brāhmans into an immeasurable mass of priestly laws and traditions, they are still greatly beloved by the people; and, unlike the Vedic literature, they may be read by women, and by men of any caste.

64. The *Bhagavadgītā* or 'Song of the Adorable', which is largely a product of Bhāgavata theology, is one of the most noteworthy pieces of literature produced in India. It is the noblest and purest expressions of modern Hinduism. The author wished to produce a poem to express his own boundless reverence for Kṛishṇa, to gather the best thoughts of the Upanishads and unite them with the most helpful parts of the philosophies, and at the same time to bind people to the ordinary life and worship of Hindu society. His book was not intended to be a class-book to be used in a Vedic school or by a few hermits in a forest, but a manual which the farmer, the soldier, the shopkeeper, and the Brāhman might read day by day, while pursuing their ordinary avocations. He did not wish to turn men into sannyāsīs, but wished to present a religious system which people might accept and use, while they continued their ordinary daily work and

lived within the caste system. The two most significant points in his teaching are the supremacy of Kṛishṇa and the theory of Karma-yoga. The significance of Kṛishṇa lies in this, that he is conceived as the absolute Brahman, the object of all the meditation of the sages of the Upanishads, and at the same time as a personal god approachable with sacrifice and prayer, like other personal gods. The significance of Karma-yoga also lies in its combination of philosophy with the popular life: as Kṛishṇa unites the loftiest meditation of the philosopher with the simplest worship of the ignorant, so Karma-yoga unites philosophic renunciation of the world with practical everyday life. The commands of Karma-yoga are: Give up all desire for the fruits of action, and thereby fulfil the philosophic ideal, but continue to do your ordinary work in the world at the same time, and thus fulfil your duty as a member of a Hindu family and caste. The author of the *Gītā* is as anxious to persuade his readers to fulfil all the rules of caste laid down in the *Dharmaśāstras*, as he is to make them rise to the philosophic contemplation of the absolute Brahman. (See section 90.) No other Hindu book has laid hold of the educated classes with the same power as the *Gītā*.

65. About the Christian era the great books of Mahāyāna Buddhism began to be written. Some of the early ones are in the vernaculars, but very soon Sanskrit comes to the front, and thereafter every great Buddhist work was written in Sanskrit. A very large literature sprang up in North India at this time. Many most famous and influential works might be mentioned, the *Questions of King Milinda*, the *Lalita Vistara*, the *Saddharma Puṇḍarīka*, the *Buddha-charita*, the *Amitāyus Sūtra*, &c. These and many of the books of the old Tripiṭaka were carried over to China and translated into Chinese by competent scholars, both Indian and Chinese.

Mahāyānists formed a canon for themselves, consisting mainly of new Mahāyāna texts but also including large parts of the old canon. In arrangement it is a Tripiṭaka also. This canon has been lost in India, but is preserved in distinct forms in Tibet and in China. The student will most readily get some idea of it by looking through Bunyiu Nanjio's *Catalogue of the Chinese Translation of the Buddhist Tripiṭaka.*

NOTE.—The text below is THE LAW AGAINST WIDOW-REMARRIAGE: 'Until death let the widow live a life of endurance, self-restraint, and chastity, yearning to fulfil the law of wives of one husband, that most excellent law.' *Mānava Dharmaśāstra*, v. 158.

आसीता मरणात्क्षान्ता नियता ब्रह्मचारिणी।
यो धर्म एकपत्नीनां काङ्क्षन्ती तमनुत्तमम॥

ILLUSTRATIVE READINGS

15. Hindu Incarnation

Kṛishṇa speaks at the battle of Kurukshetra :—

'Many births of Me and thee have passed, O Arjuna. I know them all; but thou knowest them not, O affrighter of the foe.

Though birthless and unchanging of essence, and though lord of born beings, yet in My sway over the Nature that is Mine own I come into birth by My own Magic.

For whensoever the Law fails and lawlessness uprises, O thou of Bharata's race, then do I bring Myself to bodied birth.

To guard the righteous, to destroy evil-doers, to establish the Law, I come into birth age after age.

He who knows in verity My divine birth and works comes not again to birth when he has left the body, he comes to Me, O Arjuna.

The Four Castes were created by Me according to the orders of Moods and Works; know that I am indeed the doer of that work, yet no worker, unchanging.

Father of this universe am I, mother, ordainer, grandsire, the thing that is known and the being that makes clean, the word *Om*, the Ṛik, the Sāma, and the Yajus;

The way, the supporter, the lord, the witness, the dwelling, the refuge, the friend, the origin, the dissolution, the abiding-place, the house of ward, the changeless seed.'

Bhagavadgītā, iv. 5–9, 13, ix. 17–18; Barnett, in the *Temple Classics*.

16. Buddhist Incarnation

Gautama the Buddha speaks on Gṛidhrakūṭa:—

'An inconceivable number of thousands of koṭis of Aeons, never to be measured, is it since I reached superior enlightenment and never ceased to teach the law.

I roused many Bodhisattvas and established them in Buddha-knowledge. I brought myriads of koṭis of beings, endless, to full ripeness in many koṭis of Aeons.

I show the place of extinction, I reveal to all beings a device to educate them, albeit I do not become extinct at the time, and in this very place continue preaching the law.'

'Repeatedly am I born in the world of the living.'

'What reason should I have to continually manifest myself? When men become unbelieving, unwise, ignorant, careless, fond of sensual pleasures, and from thoughtlessness run into misfortune.

Then I, who know the course of the world, declare, "I am the Tathāgata," and consider, How can I incline them to enlightenment? How can they become partakers of the Buddha-laws?

So am I the Father of the world, the Self-born, the Healer, the Protector of all creatures. Knowing them to be perverted, infatuated, and ignorant, I teach final rest, myself not being at rest.'

Saddharma Puṇḍarīka, xv. 1-3, 7, 21-23; *S.B.E.*, vol. xxi.

17. From the Vedānta Sūtras

NOTE.—A literal translation of each sūtra is given in italics, and then the meaning follows in roman.

1. *Then therefore Brahman-inquiry.*
   Here beginneth the inquiry into Brahman.

2. *Whence the birth, &c., of this.*
   Brahman is that from which the creation, preservation, and destruction of this world proceed.

3. *From being the source of Scripture.*
   The omniscience of Brahman follows from its being the source of Scripture.

4. *But that from immediate connexion.*
   But that Brahman is to be known from Scripture, because it is connected with the Upanishads as their purport.

5. *From seeing not, unscriptural.*
   On account of seeing (i. e. thinking) being attributed in the Upanishads to the cause of the world, the *pradhāna* of the Sāṅkhya philosophy is not to be identified with the cause indicated by the Upanishads; for it is not founded on Scripture.

6. *If figurative, no, from word Self.*
   If it be said that the word 'seeing' is used figuratively, we deny that, on account of the word Self being applied to the cause of the world.

Bādarāyaṇa, *Vedānta Sūtras*, I. i. 1–6.

TABLES

16. Chronology of the Incarnation Period

External Events	*History and Religion*	*Literature*		
184 B.C.	184 B.C. Fall of Aśokan Empire	Second Stage of *Mahābhārata*	Books I and VII of *Rāmāyaṇa*	
100 B.C.	Images in Buddhism 72 Fall of Śuṅga Dynasty			
44 Caesar murdered 31 Augustus supreme				
29 Christ crucified			MAHĀYĀNA LEADERS	
The New Testament	Gondophares Kanishka		Aśvaghosha	Gradual Translation of Buddhist Books into Chinese
A.D. 100		Third Stage of *Mahābhārata*	Nāgārjuna	
A.D. 200	Kṛishṇa as the Ātman	The *Gītā*		
Christianity in Malabar		*Mānava Dharma-śāstra*	Āryadeva	
A.D. 300				
Constantine grants Christians toleration, A.D. 320				

17. The Six Orthodox Systems of Hindu Philosophy

A.

1. The *Karma Mīmāṁsā*, 'work inquiry', the philosophy of sacrifice, founded on the Śrauta Sūtras. Jaimini wrote the main treatise, the *Karma Mīmāṁsā Sūtras.*

2. The *Uttara Mīmāṁsā*, 'later inquiry', the philosophy of the Upanishads, the Vedānta, systematized by Bādarāyaṇa in his work known as the *Vedānta Sūtras*, the *Brahma Sūtras*, or the *Śārīraka Sūtras.*

B.

3. The *Sāṅkhya*, a dualistic atheism, ascribed to the early sage Kapila. No early treatise survives.

4. The *Yoga.* In this system the Sāṅkhya metaphysic is combined with a personal God and with bodily and mental exercises called *yoga.* Patañjali, of the second century B.C., is the author of the manual, which is called the *Yoga Sūtras.*

C.

5. The *Vaiśeshika.* This system classifies all phenomena under logical categories, and attributes the origin of the world to atoms. The author of the manual, which is known as the *Vaiśeshika Sūtras*, is remembered by the nickname Kaṇāda, 'atom-eater'.

6. The *Nyāya* accepts the metaphysic of the Vaiśeshika, and adds a very detailed and acute exposition of formal logic. The manual, which is by Gautama, is called the *Nyāya Sūtras.*

18. Buddhas, Incarnations, and Tīrthakaras

Buddhas	*Avatāras of Vishṇu*		*Tīrthakaras*
Mythical:—			
Dīpaṁkara			
Koṇḍañña			Ṛishabhadeva
Maṅgala	*Matsya[1]:	the Fish	Ajitanātha
Sumanas	*Kūrma:	the Tortoise	Sambhavanātha
Revata	*Varāha:	the Boar	Abhinandana
Sobhita	*Narasiṁha:	the Man-lion	Sumatinātha
Anomadassin	*Vāmana:	the Dwarf	Padmaprabha
Paduma	*Paraśu-Rāma		Supārśvanātha
Nārada	*Rāma		Chandraprabha
Padumuttara	*Kṛishṇa		Ṣuvidhinātha
Sumedha	Vyāsa		Ṣitalanātha
Sujāta	Prithu		Śreyāṁsanātha
Piyadassin	Hari		Vāsupūjya
Atthadassin	Haṁsa		Vimalanātha
Dhammadassin	Manvantara		Anantanātha
Siddhattha	Yajña		Dharmanātha
Tissa	Ṛishabha		Śāntinātha
Pussa	Hayagrīva		Kunthunātha
Vipassin	Dhruva		Aranātha
Sikhin	Dhanvantari		Mallinātha
Vessabhū	Nara and Nārāyaṇa		Munisuvrata
Kakusandha	Dattātreya		Naminātha
Koṇāgamana	Kapila		Neminātha
Kassapa	Sanaka		Pārśvanātha
Historical:—			
Gautama	*Buddha[2]		Mahāvīra
Future:—			
Maitreya	*Kalki		

[1] The ten *avatāras* of Vishṇu which are usually met with are marked with asterisks.

[2] The Buddha *avatāra* of Vishṇu is really Gautama, the historical Buddha. One of the many means employed by Hindus to overcome Buddhism was to recognize the Buddha as a Hindu incarnation.

नमस्तुङ्गशिरश्चुम्बिचन्द्रचामरचारवे।
त्रैलोक्यनगरारम्भमूलस्तम्भाय शंभवे॥

CHAPTER VIII

PERIOD OF DECADENCE

THE GUPTAS: THE PURĀṆAS

From the Rise of the Guptas to the Fall of Harsha's Empire. A.D. 320–650

66. *History*. Our period opens with the rise of the great dynasty of the Guptas, who during the earlier part of their rule reigned at Patna, but later moved up to Ayodhyā. Under their empire North India enjoyed a period of really good government, worthy of comparison with the time of Aśoka. The two greatest kings of the dynasty were Samudragupta and Chandragupta II Vikramāditya. The latter king conquered Mālwā and probably lived from time to time in Ujjain; so that he may be the reality behind all the mythical tales told about the great Vikramāditya of Ujjain.

67. This dynasty went down before the attacks of the Huns. These Mongol invaders behaved with monstrous cruelty and violence during the fifty years they were in India. They destroyed Patna. They sacked Buddhist

NOTE.—The text at the top of the page is a couplet IN PRAISE OF ŚIVA: 'Adoration to Śambhu, adorned with the chowrie-like moon on his lofty brow, main pillar in the building of the city of the three worlds!' First couplet of Bāṇa's *Harshacharita*.

monasteries, massacred the monks, and even killed the Patriarch. They were driven out, however, in A. D. 528; and from that time onward until the invasions of Mahmūd of Ghaznī about A. D. 1000, India was comparatively free from foreign attack.

68. About A. D. 550 a powerful dynasty known as the Chālukyas arose at Bādāmi in Dharwār and played a great

18. THE TRIMŪRTI

The Hindu Triad, representing Brahmā, Vishṇu, and Śiva as one. A most powerful piece of sculpture, cut in the solid rock of the cave of Elephanta, near Bombay, dating from about A. D. 800. (Photograph by Clifton & Co., Bombay.)

part in South Indian politics and civilization for two centuries; while on the other coast at Kāñchī, now Conjeeveram, the Pallavas ruled the surrounding country.

69. During the seventh century another brilliant figure appears in North India, the famous Harsha of Kanauj. He spent many years in conquest, and finally was the acknowledged sovereign of the whole of North India from the Himalayas to the Nerbudda. He was fortunate in having at his court a distinguished literary man named Bāṇa, who wrote an historical romance setting forth the great deeds of his patron. We also hear a good deal about him from the Chinese traveller Hiouen Tsang, who was greatly honoured by him. Our period closes with his empire.

70. *Religion.* Hinduism during this period is chiefly

19. THE MARRIAGE OF ŚIVA AND PĀRVATĪ
A very fine piece of work, but badly damaged. Also at Elephanta.
(Photograph by Clifton & Co., Bombay.)

marked by a coarse noisy sectarianism with little dignity or morality in it. The follower of Śiva or of Vishṇu uses the most extravagant language in praising his own God and curses the devotees of the other heartily. An attempt was made to reconcile all sectaries by the doctrine of the threefold manifestation of the Supreme in Brahmā, Vishṇu, and Śiva; but the concept never truly laid hold of the Hindu people. The Triad is frequently mentioned, and it is now and then represented in sculpture; but it was Śiva and Vishṇu that drew the reverence of men. The mythology of the time is wild and extravagant, and there is but little seriousness in the teaching. The Purāṇas (see section 72) are full of bombast and pretentiousness.

In this period the myths about Kṛishṇa underwent considerable embellishment. The story of his childhood was told in great detail, several points being borrowed, as it seems, from Christian sources. His cowherd exploits also took form at this time and captured the masses. All this fresh mythology had its centre in Mathurā and Vṛindāvana. Clearly the cult of Kṛishṇa was carried on there with great fervour.

20. BUDDHIST IMAGE

From Java. In Calcutta Museum. Note the great halo.

Hinduism and Buddhism drew nearer and nearer to each other during those centuries, each borrowing from the other, both becoming steadily coarser, but Hinduism continuously gaining in popularity. It was a period of marked decadence; but Hinduism had by far the stronger constitution.

71. This period saw a very great expansion of Buddhism in other lands. It became supreme in China; and throughout the period numerous Indian scholars went to China to teach the faith, while many Chinese pilgrims found their way to India. The translation of Buddhist texts into Chinese went on apace, both Indians and Chinese doing large service in this way. From China the religion passed into Korea and Japan. Devoted missionaries carried it to Burma, Siam, and Java, and won the populations of those

lands. Its influence spread far and wide over the whole of Central and Eastern Asia. India was its home, and there its most famous scholars studied and taught. The greatest University of Buddhism, Nālandā in Bihār, was founded during the sixth century, and was adorned by a long succession of great scholars for at least two centuries thereafter. The philosophy of Buddhism at this time shows a great approximation to Hindu thought.

21. ROCK-CUT SHRINE

At Mahāvellipore. A reference to fig. 1 will show that the design is copied from a hut. But the interest of the form is this, that it seems to be the origin of the curvilinear tower of the Indo-Aryan style. Imagine the centre of the roof raised, and the lines of the Indo-Aryan tower are at once realized. (See figs. 22 and 28.)

72. *Literature, &c.* The Guptas were great patrons of literature. The earliest existing Purāṇas, which embody the sectarian religion of the period, seem to date from their time; and every branch of secular literature rose to splendour under their fostering care, the Drama, Kāvya poetry, Rhetoric, Grammar, Astronomy, Romance. The word *Purāṇa* means *archaeologica*, and was first used of old-world myths and tales about the origin of things. The existing Purāṇas, however, are sectarian pamphlets in Sanskrit verse, written to catch the popular ear and secure worshippers for Vishṇu, Śiva, or Brahmā. Each begins with an account of the origin of the world, but soon becomes a panegyric of the favourite divinity. Men of

any caste, and women too, are allowed to read the Purāṇas.

Buddhist literature at this time consisted mostly of philosophic works produced by the scholars of Nālandā.

The Śvetāmbara Jain canon received its final form in A. D. 454.

73. During this period architecture was cultivated with zeal and success by Buddhists, Jains, and Hindus. A great deal of the finest cave-work dates from this time. Very few buildings, however, belonging to these centuries remain above ground. Yet one of the most beautiful, the great Buddhist pagoda at Buddh-Gayā, has survived, though probably much altered. The rich cluster of Hindu temples at Bhuvaneśvara in Orissa are also still standing. They are of the Indo-Aryan style.

22. TEMPLE OF MUKTEŚVARA

At Bhuvaneśvara. A small but beautiful shrine of the Indo-Aryan style. The ornamental arch in front, called a Toraṇa, is very graceful. (Photograph kindly favoured by Mr. Frank Anderson, of Bombay.)

A Hindu or Jain temple consists of a cubical cell, lighted only from the door, but surmounted by a tower. The image is placed in the cell, which thus becomes the shrine. The tower marks the position of the shrine. Usually a porch stands in front of the door of the shrine.

The three leading styles are distinguished from each other by the form of the tower. The Northern or Indo-Aryan tower has curvilinear sides: see figs. 22 and 28. The Southern or Dravidian tower is pyramidal and in stories: see figs. 23 and 34. The Chālukyan tower is usually star-shaped: see fig. 29. The earliest existing examples of Dravidian architecture are the Pallava temples of Conjeeveram and the rock-cut monuments known as the Seven

23. ROCK-CUT SHRINE

At Mahāvellipore. This and the other shrines, known as the Seven Pagodas, are all Hindu work. But the style of this example is taken unchanged from a Buddhist *vihāra* or monastery. Then this in turn produced the tower of the Dravidian style. (See figs. 21 and 28.)

Pagodas at Mahāvellipore near Madras, which date from the seventh century. About the same time the Chālukyan style arose in the West.

NOTE.—The text at the bottom of the page is an example of Purāṇic intolerance: 'Vishṇu is the divinity of the gods; the Trident-holder (i. e. Śiva) is the divinity of devils.' *Kūrma Purāṇa*, xxii. 43.

देवानां दैवतं विष्णुर्दानवानां त्रिशूलधृक् ॥

ILLUSTRATIVE READINGS

18. Vishṇu as Saviour of the Gods

An Example of Purāṇic Mythology

The gods addressed the mighty Vishṇu thus—
'Conquered in battle by the evil demons,
We fly to thee for succour, Soul of all:
Pity and by thy might deliver us.'
Hari the lord, creator of the world,
Thus by the gods implored, all graciously
Replied—'Your strength shall be restored, ye gods;
Only accomplish what I now command;
Unite yourselves in peaceful combination
With these your foes; collect all plants and herbs
Of diverse kinds from every quarter; cast them
Into the sea of milk; take Mandara,
The mountain, for a churning-stick, and Vāsuki,
The serpent, for a rope; together churn
The ocean to produce the beverage—
Source of all strength and immortality;
Then reckon on my aid. I will take care
Your foes shall share your toil, but not partake
In its reward or drink th' immortal draught';
Thus by the god of gods advised, the host
United in alliance with the demons.
Straightway they gathered various herbs and cast them
Into the waters, then they took the mountain
To serve as churning-staff, and next the snake
To serve as cord, and in the ocean's midst
Hari himself, present in tortoise-form,
Became a pivot for the churning-staff.

Vishṇu Purāṇa, i. 9; Monier-Williams, *Indian Wisdom*, 498.

19. Living Souls in Particles of Earth

NOTE.—This extract is inserted here as an example of the characteristic teaching of the Jains. Similar statements follow in the same *Sūtra* with reference to living souls in fire, water, and air.

The living world is afflicted, miserable, difficult to instruct, and without discrimination. In this world full of pain, suffering by their different acts, see the benighted ones cause great pain. See! there are beings individually embodied in earth; not one all-soul. See! there are men who control themselves, whilst others only pretend to be houseless, i. e. monks such as the Buddhists, whose conduct differs not from that of householders, because one destroys this earth-body by bad and injurious doings, and many other beings besides, which he hurts by means of earth, through his doing acts relating to earth.

As somebody may cut or strike a blind man who cannot see the wound; as somebody may cut or strike the foot, the ankle, the knee, the thigh, the hip, the navel, the belly, the flank, the back, the bosom, the heart, the breast, the neck, the arm, the finger, the nail, the eye, the brow, the forehead, the head; as some kill openly; as some extirpate secretly; thus the earth-bodies are cut, struck, and killed, though their feeling is not manifest. He who injures these earth-bodies does not comprehend and renounce the sinful acts; he who does not injure these, comprehends and renounces the sinful acts. Knowing them, a wise man should not act sinfully towards earth, nor cause others to act so, nor allow others to act so. He who knows these causes of sin relating to earth, is called a reward-knowing sage. Thus I say.

Āchārāṅga Sūtra, I, i. 2, 1–2, 5–6; *S.B.E.*, vol. xxii, 3–5.

TABLES

19. Period of Decadence

External Events	*History and Religion*	*Literature*	
Buddhism enters Korea A.D. 400	A.D. 320 Rise of the Guptas A.D. 326 Samudragupta A.D. 375 Chandragupta II	*Vāyu Purāṇa*	BUDDHIST
A.D. 500	The Iron Pillar at Delhi The Huns Fall of the Gupta Empire	Kālidāsa Jain Śvetāmbara canon fixed A.D. 454	SCHOLARS Buddhaghosha
A.D. 552 Buddhism in Japan A.D. 600	Pāṭaliputra destroyed A.D. 528 Defeat of the Huns	Early Purāṇas edited HINDU ARCHITECTURE	Asaṅga Vasubandhu Dignāga
Muhammad 570–632 Buddhism in Tibet, Siam, Burma and Java	Harsha reigns A.D. 606–647 Hiouen Tsang in India A.D. 629–646 Persian cross at Kottayam	Rājputāna Bādāmi Conjeeveram Mahāvellipore Bhuvaneśvara	Guṇaprabha Dharmakīrti

20. The Leading Divinities of the Hindu Pantheon

The incomprehensible *Brahman* is manifested in the Triad—*Brahmā, Vishṇu, Śiva.*

Brahman

- *Brahmā*, the Creator, married Sarasvatī, the goddess of learning.
- *Vishṇu*, the Preserver, married Lakshmī, the goddess of wealth, called also Śrī.
- *Śiva*, the Destroyer, married Umā, the daughter of Himālaya. She is also called Pārvatī, Durgā, Kālī, Bhavānī.

Their sons are *Gaṇeśa*, the elephant-headed god, whose functions are somewhat like those of the Roman Janus, and *Kārttikeya*, called also *Subrahmaṇya*, *Skanda* and *Kumāra*, the god of war.

என்னை ஆளுடையாய்! சிற்றுயிர்க்
கிரங்கிக், காய்சின ஆலமுண்டாய்! அமு
துண்ணக் கடையவனே!

CHAPTER IX

PERIOD OF RECONSTRUCTION

POET-SAINTS AND COMMENTATORS

From the Fall of Harsha's Empire to the Conquest of North India. A.D. 650–1200

74. *History*. There are very few outstanding events in the dead, dull level of these five and a half centuries. Muḥammadan aggression was almost entirely confined to Sind and the frontier until the latter part of the twelfth century. Yet great ethnic changes were going on. The foreign races which had entered India in the earlier centuries, and the aboriginal races of Bengal and Bihār which had risen to prominence, were gradually absorbed and assimilated by the old Hindu people. Numerous tribes were transformed into castes, and their leaders were supplied with a mythical genealogy. From the midst of this creative chaos arose the Rājputs and dominated the centre and the west for several centuries. They were a chivalrous

NOTE.—The lines at the top of the page form ONE OF MĀṆIKKA VĀCHAKAR'S GREAT SAYINGS about Śiva: 'Thou mad'st me thine; didst fiery poison eat, pitying poor souls, that I might thine ambrosia taste—I, meanest one.' *Tiruvāchakam*, Pope, p. 102.

race, and their kingdoms in Mālwā, Delhi, Kanauj, Ājmīr, and Gwālior showed great activity, military courage and high civilization; but their dissensions made them an easy prey, when the bold Muḥammadan invaders came. In the south a number of kingdoms arose and flourished and fell; and the local fortunes of Jainism, of Buddhism, or of some Hindu sect were frequently intertwined with the

24. Jain Sculpture

Illustrating the worship of the Digambara Jains, at Kalugumalai, Tinnevelly. See section 48. (Photograph by Nicholas & Co., Madras.

political change; but these events can scarcely be traced in a primer.

75. *Religion and Literature.* The steady rise of Hinduism to supremacy and the corresponding decline of Buddhism are the most prominent features of the religious history of this period.

But when we look more closely, we become aware that a subtle change has passed over Hindu faith and practice.

Modern Hinduism has been born. The ancient Vedic sacrifices have fallen almost altogether into disuse. It is the worship of the temples and the annual festivals celebrated at home that hold the affections of the people. Where

25. TEMPLE OF ŚIVA AT TANJORE

This fine stone edifice is Dravidian in style: see section 73. It was built by Rājarāja the Great, a Choḷa king, about A.D. 1000. (Photograph by Wiele & Klein, Madras.)

philosophic influence is strong, animal sacrifices are prohibited in the temples; but in many places the practice has come in once more, along with many new divinities, from the aboriginal peoples. Processions and shows and dramatic representations are common. Prostitutes are kept in most temples as servants of the god.

Another conception seems to have taken shape in our period, the idea that each goddess is the *śakti* or energy of her husband. The god is conceived as retired, absolute, inconceivable: the goddess is a sort of emanation from him, bringing his power down to man, and is a much more approachable being than her lord.

The two great sects, the Vishṇuite and the Śivaite, still continue to hold the supreme place in the religion throughout our period. Their systems of worship are now completely developed. The chief difference between Śaiva and Vaishṇava worship is this, that Śiva is usually represented by the phallic symbol, the *liṅga* and the *yoni*, while Vishṇu is always represented by an image. The ritual differs in details, but only in details. Vaishṇavas never sacrifice animals, and the same is true of all Śaivas in South India. The usual offerings are grain, fruit, flowers, and milk. Both sects give *tīrtha* and *prasāda* to their worshippers, i. e. a portion of the water and of the food which have been offered to the idol.

Both use sect-marks on the forehead and other parts of the body; but the Vaishṇavas, in addition, brand on the body the symbols of Vishṇu. Both sects pay worship to their teachers, *gurus*, and lay great stress on their ministrations. Both use a *mantra* or watchword, to which they attribute great supernatural power. Both appeal to men of all castes; yet both uphold the laws of caste with great rigidness.

During this period a third sect of great importance arose, chiefly in Bengal, the *Śāktas* or worshippers of *Kālī*, the wife of Śiva, as his *śakti*. They fall into two groups, the right-hand and the left-hand Śāktas. Both groups show many signs of aboriginal influence, notably animal sacrifice and magic rites; and the basis of the whole cult in both is phallic; but, while the right-hand group are respectable in their worship, the left-hand Śāktas are most immoral. Their cult is based on the five M's, or elements of worship the Sanskrit names of which begin with M, flesh, wine,

26. LIṄGA SHRINE

This shrine is within the cave temple hollowed out of the solid rock in the island of Elephanta, in Bombay Harbour. See fig. 18. The figures are *dvārapālas*, door-wardens, keeping the entrance of Śiva's residence. (From a postcard.)

women, fish, and finger-signs. In other points Śāktas are like Śivaites.

76. These sects naturally required manuals describing their worship and sectarian practices. The earliest of these books, which take the place occupied in Vedic worship by the Śrauta-sūtras, appeared early in this period. Vaishṇava manuals are called *Pāñcharātra Saṁhitās*, Śaiva manuals *Śaiva Agamas*, and Śākta manuals *Tantras*. This literature

is in Sanskrit, and most of it is in verse. In many respects these books are like the Purāṇas.

About the same time Buddhism in Bengal and Bihār yielded to the attractions of *śakti*-worship and magic, and developed Tāntric thought and practice. A University filled with this spirit arose at Vikramaśila on the Ganges. Tibet accepted this form of the faith and still remains true to it.

77. The twelve *Āḻvārs* (often called *Azhvārs*: they were wandering teachers and poets of various castes) preached in South India a popular Vishṇuism, which drew its inspiration from the Purāṇic stories of Kṛishṇa. They offered salvation through Vishṇu to men of any caste. They caught the ear of the people with their beautiful Tamil hymns. These were finally gathered in a collection, the name of which is the *Nālāyira Prabandham*, but which is often referred to as the Tamil Veda. These popular lyrics are still used in the daily worship of most of the Vishṇuite temples of the south.

78. Contemporaneously the *Aḍiyārs* did a similar service for the religion of Śiva. The three greatest of them were Appar, Ñāna Sambandhar, and Sundarar. Their Tamil hymns form the *Devāram*, or 'Divine Garland', and have exercised a great influence on Śaivism. Like the Vishṇuites, they offered salvation to all. In the tenth century a still greater man, known as *Māṇikka Vāchakar*, consecrated his poetic gifts to Śiva. He wrote a collection of exquisite Tamil lyrics which form the *Tiruvāchakam*, or Sacred Utterance. Both these collections of hymns are used in the worship of Śiva in the temples.

79. In North India the *Bhāgavata Purāṇa* or Purāṇa of the Adorable, a rhapsody on Kṛishṇa, and by far the most influential of the Purāṇas, appeared somewhere about the tenth century. Nimbārka, whose followers worship Rādhā, Kṛishṇa's cowherd mistress, as well as Kṛishṇa himself, came

a little later. Jayadeva, the author of the *Gītā Govinda*, or Cowherd Song, which celebrates Kṛishṇa in the richest

27. ŚIVA THE DANCER, NAṬARĀJA

Śiva's activity in the world and in the soul is spoken of as sport, and is symbolized in his dance. (V. Smith, *Indian Art*, fig. 174.)

erotic strain, flourished about A. D. 1100. The *Bhakti-sūtra* of Śāṇḍilya is a non-sectarian philosophic work, defining the Bhāgavata doctrine. All these books are in Sanskrit.

At Kalyān in the Marāṭhā country in the twelfth century, Basava, the prime minister of the state, founded the Vīra Śaiva sect. The movement seems to have been essentially a revolt against Brāhman domination. The ancient worship

28. TEMPLE OF JAGANNĀTH AT PURĪ, ORISSA

A Vishṇuite shrine of Indo-Aryan style. Note that there are three porches, each with a pyramidal roof. The curvilinear tower, marking the situation of the shrine, stands out behind. The date is about A. D. 1100. (Photograph by Wiele & Klein, Madras.)

of Śiva is retained, only the *liṅga* and Śiva's bull, Nandi, are very prominent. Members of the sect are distinguished from ordinary Hindus by the wearing of a small *liṅga* somewhere about the person. Hence they are commonly called Liṅgāyats. Their priests are called Jaṅgamas. At first they renounced caste completely; but the old poison has crept in amongst them again, and they demand recognition for their caste distinctions in the census papers. Caste had been denounced earlier by Kapilar and Vemana, the first a Tamil, the second a Telugu poet; but the Vīra Śaiva sect

29. CHĀLUKYAN TEMPLE

At Somnāthpur, in Mysore. The star-shaped tower may be distinctly seen. Part of the porch with its pierced slabs of stone is visible also. (See p. 104.) The date is about A. D. 1050.

seems to have been the earliest organized movement that opposed the ancient basis of Hindu society. Similar attempts followed in North India. (See section 91.)

80. *Bhakti* is one of the most important elements of the teaching of all these sects. *Bhakti* means 'adoration' directed towards Bhagavān, 'the adorable,' by the Bhakta, 'the adoring devotee.' Bhagavān is used of Vishṇu, Kṛishṇa, Rāma, Śiva, or any other god the worshipper adores. All the modern *bhakti* schools of Vishṇuism are called by the common name of Bhāgavatas, worshippers of Bhagavān. This, as we saw in section 56, was the name of a very early Vishṇuite school.

81. This is also the period of the great *āchāryas* or systematic teachers. Each was a sannyāsī, and was either the head of a school or the chief priest of a sect. They distinguished themselves by writing, teaching, preaching, and public disputation. Their writings, which are in Sanskrit, are largely commentaries on the sacred books, both *śruti* and *smṛiti*; but they did large service also in combating Buddhism and Jainism, and some of them were great organizers as well.

The *Karma Mīmāṁsā* and the *Vedānta* (see p. 96) were the supreme schools of the time. The other four philosophies had their followers, but they were of comparatively little account. Every sect seems to have accepted Bādarāyaṇa's *Vedānta-sūtras* as an authoritative work.

The first of these famous āchāryas is Kumārila, who represents the *Karma Mīmāṁsā* school. He flourished about A. D. 700, and wrote a commentary on the sūtras of Jaimini.

A little more than a century later there appeared the great Śaṅkara (A. D. 788 to about 850), the supreme āchārya of the Vedānta school. His fame rests on his commentaries on the *Vedānta-sūtras*, the *Bhagavadgītā*, and the chief Upanishads. He held that the true Vedānta system was *advaita*, i. e. an unqualified monism. Nothing is real except Brahman. Man's soul is the eternal spirit whole and undivided; and the world is *māyā*, illusion. Henceforward the central school of the Vedānta is *advaita*, strictly monistic. His scholarship and immense capacity secured him great influence; and his system of thought was accepted all over India.

From this time onward the central school of the Vedānta accepts the doctrine of incarnations taught in the *Gītā*.

30. IMAGE OF ŚAṄKARA IN THE KĀMĀCHĪAMMA TEMPLE, BIG CONJEEVERAM

Note the single rod (see section 109) and the pose of the great teacher's right hand. The smaller image in front represents Śaṅkara also. It is carried in processions, but the great image is never moved. (Photographed for the author.)

Thus the ancient philosophy attached to itself a theology with the worship of a personal god and the use of idols. Śaṅkara seems also to have accepted and taught the doctrine of the Hindu triad in the philosophic form, viz. that Brahmā,

Vishṇu, and Śiva are the triple manifestation of the impersonal One, but that they are not eternal beings. This is the theology of the Smārta Brāhmans of South India. But he did a very great work also by his preaching in all parts of India, by his opposition to the sects that swarmed in his day, by re-arranging the ascetic orders and by the foundation of a number of monasteries for the encouragement of learning, formed on the model of Buddhist monasteries.

But the theistic sects, although they recognized the *Vedānta-sūtras* as an inspired work, found it hard to square the monistic metaphysic and impersonal theology of Śaṅkara with their religious beliefs.

It was nearly three centuries later before the worshippers of Vishṇu produced a man fit to wrestle with Śaṅkara over this great question. Their protagonist is Rāmānuja, whose mean date is A.D. 1100. He carried on the work of the Āḻvārs, and was high-priest of the whole Vaishṇava community of the south. His commentary on the *Vedānta-sūtras* is known as the *Śrī-bhāshya*, and has achieved a popularity almost as great as the work of Śaṅkara. He calls his system *viśishṭādvaita*, modified monism, and claims that it is the true Vedānta, the doctrine of the Upanishads. Brahman is Vishṇu and is personal. Man's spirit is an *aṁśa* or portion of God, and even in final union retains its own individuality and consciousness. The doctrine of incarnations is strongly held.

On one point he held a very ambiguous position. As a Vedāntist he could speak only to twice-born men; for they only had the right to read the Upanishads. Further, his system was a burdensome one in its rules about eating, bathing, and dressing. But, on the other hand, as the heir of the Āḻvārs, who had preached to all classes of men, he taught the common people Vaishṇavism, and even admitted the outcastes on occasion to certain temples.

A century later his followers fell into two sects, the northern school, *Vaḍa-galai*, and the southern school, *Teṅ-galai*. The chief difference between them lies in the doctrine of the influence of divine grace on the soul, the northern school

31. BRONZE IMAGE OF RĀMĀNUJA AT ŚRĪPERUMBŪDŪR

This image is said to have been consecrated during Rāmānuja's lifetime in the temple of his native place, and may therefore be a portrait. Note the sect-mark on the forehead, the triple rod (see section 109), and the symbol in front, which represents Śaṭhakopa, the great Āḷvār. See p. 129. (The author owes this photograph to the courtesy of Mr. A. Govindāchārya Svāmī, of Mysore City.)

teaching that it is 'Co-operative', the southern that it is 'Irresistible'. Both hold the doctrine of *bhakti*, 'love, faith, adoration,' and also the doctrine of *prapatti*, 'surrender,' but the southern section make this latter a passive, involuntary resignation correspondent to the irresistible grace of God.

Hence the former is called the Monkey school, because the young monkey clings to his mother, while the latter is the Cat school, because the kitten is carried by the mother.

The āchārya of the worshippers of Śiva is Nīlakaṇṭha. In his commentary on the *Vedānta-sūtras* he claims that Brahman is Śiva and is personal, and that the soul is distinct from God. Yet the system is called *advaita*, i.e. monistic, the monism being explained in the sense that the individual, though distinct, is inseparable from God, and that when at last the man, achieving Release, approaches God, 'he wears away atom by atom, so that at the moment of union nothing of him is left, and what is left is the Presence of the Supreme One only and the feeling of His Presence, and no feeling, or consciousness of feeling, of himself or others.' The whole doctrine of incarnations is denied, but instead of it there is the doctrine that Śiva manifests himself in various forms to his worshippers.

It is most noticeable that these philosophic leaders, though they were sannyāsīs and Vedāntists, yet lived in the closest co-operation with the temple-worship of the time. They worshipped images, and are themselves represented by images and worshipped to-day in numerous temples throughout India.

82. During these centuries all the great centres of population were adorned with splendid temples covered with the most delicate and elaborate sculpture, though here and there horribly defiled by indecency.

83. It was during this period that the custom of burning a widow along with her husband's body became common and was recognized as right. The woman who dares this great act of devotion is highly praised in the *Garuḍa Purāṇa*; and by common consent she was called a *satī*, emphatically a 'good' woman. Hence the modern name of the custom. At the same time it became customary to demand that the widow who would not ascend her husband's pyre should henceforward live a life ot asceticism and privation.

32. GOPURAMS

Of temple of Śiva at Tanjore. A Dravidian temple usually stands in a large courtyard, the entrance to which is under a massive gateway called a Gopuram. Early examples such as these are of stone and are moderate in height. (Photograph by Wiele & Klein, Madras.)

NOTE.—The text below is in favour of WIDOW-BURNING: 'If a woman's husband dies, let her lead a life of chastity, or else mount his pyre.' *Vishṇusmṛiti*, xxv. 14.

मृते भर्तरि ब्रह्मचर्यं तदन्वारोहणं वा ॥

ILLUSTRATIVE READINGS

20. The Praise of Śiva in Tamil

NOTE.—This is an extract from one of the hymns of Appar, one of the Śaiva Aḍiyārs. (See pp. 114 and 143.)

Ritualism Valueless.

From hold of moral blame and sin,
O ye who would be truly free!
Adore the holy feet of Him,
Our Dancing Lord, and think of Him
With love and joy. The Watcher will
With you abiding grant His grace.

What though ye be great doctors wise?
What though ye hear the *śāstras* read?
What though the duty ye assume
Of doling out cooked food and gifts?
What though ye know the eight and two?
It boots him naught who does not feel
The noble truth that God is love.

What though ye roam through lands and wilds?
What though ye faultless penance make?
What though ye give up eating meat
And heav'nward look? None wins reward
But those that praise the knowing Lord.

What though your views are proper, true?
What though ye fast? Upon a hill
What though ye make a penance great?
What though ye bathe and show you fair?
It boots none aught but those that feel
That all through time the Lord endures.

Translated by J. M. Nallasvāmi Piḷḷai.

21. The Praise of Vishṇu in Tamil

NOTE.—These are two short extracts from the hymns of the greatest of the Ālvārs, who is known as Nammālvār, or Śaṭhakopa. (See p. 129.)

(a) *The Love of God and of the World.*

My Father, Lord of worlds evolved, involved, breathes there the man
That sees thy lotus feet with royal signs adorned, which stride
The triple worlds at once, and seeing will not melt away
In bliss ambrosial sweet, his heart immersed in joy supreme,
A sweetness ravishing, a sense sublime?—If so, ah fool!
He knows not, what for him is highest good, pure love for Thee!
Ah fool, to lose this wealth, and strain his every nerve to win
With mountain-labour short-lived joy or power o'er mortal things,
Ev'n if he sways the triad spheres, or sleeps in heaven's shade.

(b) *A Prayer for Release from Transmigration.*

Eternal Lord of angels, who dost deign to veil Thy form
In all Creation's varied state, to save poor souls,
Vouchsafe in all Thy grace to stay and hear Thy servants' cry,
That we be saved the dire return to former wretchedness,
When we mistook the body for the soul, and sinned all sins,
Which clung to us and fixed us evermore to mortal frames.

From A. Govindāchārya, *The Holy Lives of the Āzhvārs*, pp. 220–1.

22. Extract from a Commentary

NOTE.—This passage is given here to show the style of the great commentator, Śaṅkara. It is also of interest as expressing the relation of the famous work, the *Vedānta-sūtras*, to the Vedānta-texts, as the Upanishads are here called.

Some of those who maintain a Lord to be the cause of the world, think that the existence of a Lord different from mere transmigrating beings can be inferred by means of the argument stated just now without recourse being had to Scripture at all.—But, it might be said, you yourself in the Sūtra under discussion have merely brought forward the same argument! —By no means, we reply. The Sūtras, i.e. literally 'the strings', have merely the purpose of stringing together the flowers of the Vedānta-passages. In reality the Vedānta-passages referred to by the Sūtras are discussed here. For the comprehension of Brahman is effected by the ascertainment, consequent on discussion, of the sense of the Vedānta-texts, not either by inference or by the other means of right knowledge. While, however, the Vedānta-passages primarily declare the cause of the origin, &c., of the world, inference also, being an instrument of right knowledge in so far as it does not contradict the Vedānta-texts, is not to be excluded as a means of confirming the meaning ascertained. Scripture itself, moreover, allows argumentation; for the passages, *Bṛihadāraṇyaka Upanishad*, II. iv. 5, and *Chhāndogya Upanishad*, VI. xiv. 2, declare that human understanding assists Scripture.

Śaṅkara's *Bhāshya* to the *Vedānta-Sūtras*, I. i. 2; *S.B.E.*, vol. xxxiv. p. 17.

23. Sūtras on the Nature of Bhakti

1. Now then there is a wish to know faith (i.e. *bhakti*).

2. In its highest form it is an affection fixed on God.

3. From the promise of immortality to him who abides in Him.

4. If you say, it is knowledge—no, because the knowledge of one who hates Him is not an abiding in Him.

5. And from its inferiority thereto.

6. It is an affection from its being the opposite of hatred and from the Vedic expression 'taste'.

7. It is not an action; for, like knowledge, it does not depend on effort.

8. Hence indeed is the endlessness of its fruit.

9. And from the use of the word 'resignation' (*prapatti*) in the case of one who has knowledge, as in other cases where 'resignation' is used.

10. This [faith] is the main thing, since the others depend upon it.

22. This [faith] is indeed the highest from the express declaration of its superiority to the performers of sacrificial acts, to those who follow knowledge, and to those who practise concentration.

24. But it is not the same as belief, because it has a wider range.

78. All, down even to the despised castes, are capable of learning it at second-hand, like the great common truths.

83. This [highest faith] is the true identity with the Supreme, since this is recognized as the meaning of the *Gītā*.

From Cowell's translation of Śāṇḍilya's *Bhakti-Sūtras*.

TABLES

21. Chronology of Period of Reconstruction

External Events	*History*	*Religion*	*Literature*
A.D. 700			
711 Muḥammadans in Sind 732 Europe saved from Islam A.D. 800	The Parsis arrive in India	Rock-cut Temple of Kailās at Ellora	Kumārila
A.D. 900		Second Persian cross at Kottayam Decline of Buddhism	Śaṅkara
A.D. 1000		Rise of Jainism in the South	*Bhāgavata Purāṇa* Māṇikka Vāchakar
1096 The Crusades A.D. 1100	Rājarāja the Great A.D. 1025 Temple of Somnāth destroyed	The great Temple of Tanjore	Nimbārka
A.D. 1200	Conquest of North India by Muḥammadans	A.D. 1193 Buddhism crushed in Bengal and Bihār	Rāmānuja, *Gītā Govinda*, *Bhakti Sūtra*

22. The Vaishṇavas of the South

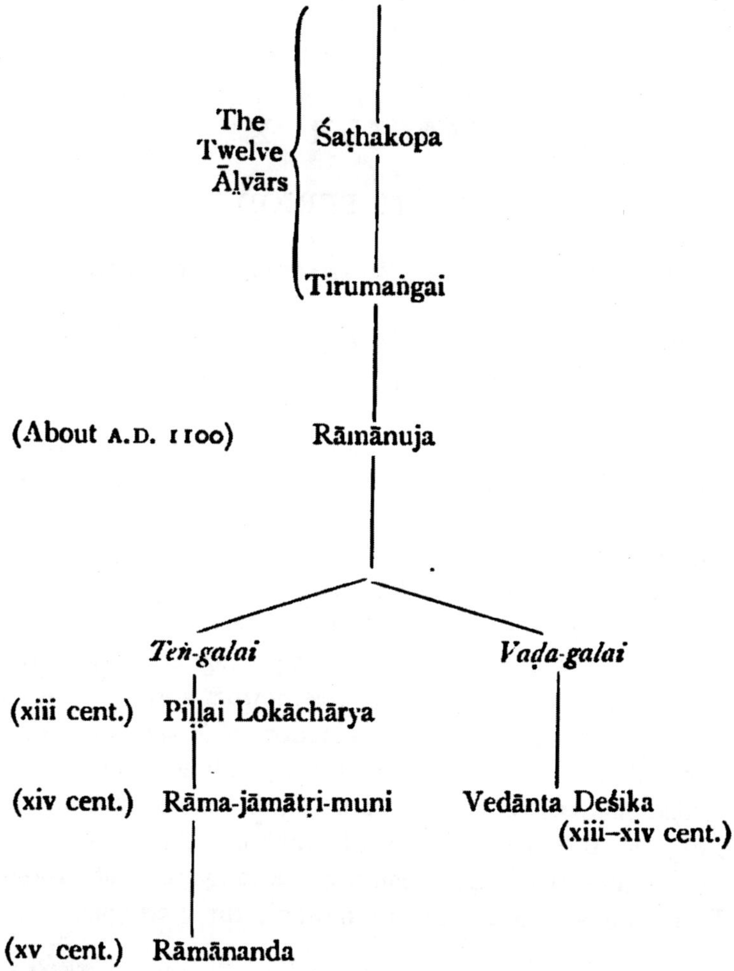

माला लकड़ देवा पत्थर गंगा जमना पानी
राम कृष्ण दोनो मर गये चारों वेद कहानी ॥

CHAPTER X

BHAKTI PERIOD

THE MUḤAMMADANS: VERNACULAR LITERATURE

From the Conquest of North India to the Battle of Plassey: A.D. 1200–1757

84. *History*. The Muḥammadan conquest of North India at the very beginning of this period, with the piece-meal conquest of Southern India during the following centuries, is practically all that the history of this period contains. The violence, bloodshed, and cruelty of the early conquests were followed by the marvellous wisdom, temperance, and justice of Akbar; but his great-grandson Aurangzeb brought back the persecuting horrors and cruelties of the earlier time. The Hindu kingdom of Vijayanagar withstood for a couple of centuries the whole force of the Muḥammadans of the Deccan, but it was overthrown in 1565, in the fierce battle of Tālikoṭ. From this time Muḥammadan influence had a wider range in South India. From the sixteenth century onward, the Portuguese, the

NOTE.—The text at the top of the page is in Hindī, and is said to be by Kabīr:—

'The beads are of wood, the gods of stone; the Ganges and the Jumna are water; Rāma and Kṛishṇa are dead; the Vedas are fictitious stories.'

Dutch, the French, and the English were to be found at many points on the seaboard of India; but not until some decades after the battle of Plassey did Europe exercise any serious influence on the life of the people.

85. *Religion and Literature.* The Muḥammadan conquest of India must not be regarded as merely a series of brilliant military exploits leading to a vast political change.

33. HINDU PILLARS IN MOSQUE

Beside Qutb Minār, Delhi. This mosque was built from the spoils of twenty-seven Hindu and Jain temples.

The conquerors regarded themselves as crusaders, attacking a vast idolatrous paganism in the name of God. Hence, wherever they went, they destroyed the religious schools, overthrew the temples, smashed the idols, drove away or killed the Buddhist monks and the Hindu priests. Idolatry was forbidden, and a tax was imposed on non-Muslims. It was their missionary method, their way of overcoming Hinduism. Muslim policy allowed but little relief or peace for the Hindu, or opportunity to rebuild, until Akbar arose. Throughout the whole vast territory in North India where their armies came and went, there is scarcely a fragment of ancient Hindu work left, except what they built into their mosques.

34. QUTB MINĀR AT DELHI
The iron pillar dates from Chandragupta II, about A. D. 415. The pillars of the mosque are Hindu and Jain. The Minār, a memorial of the Muslim conquest, dates from about A. D. 1230.

86. Buddhism seems to have disappeared almost altogether under the shock; and Hinduism suffered most severely also; for many Hindus became Muslims, and, with the fall of the Hindu kingdoms and the forfeiture of temple lands, school, monastery, and priest were left without income. Hence Sanskrit scholarship and Hindu learning made comparatively little show in North India for a very long time; but at Vijayanagar a great deal of good work was done. The commentaries of the brothers Sāyaṇa and Mādhava are of great value.

Yet Hinduism was too deeply rooted in the hearts of the people to be destroyed by adversity. Though changes necessarily arose as a result of the conquest, it is surprising how little alteration was produced in the religion. Indeed it would not be too much to say that the crushing of the Hinduism of the temple and the scholar led to the outbursting of a simpler and more helpful faith from the heart of the people itself.

35. SUBRAHMAṆYA TEMPLE AT TANJORE

(Photograph by Wiele & Klein.)

87. The Muslims were later in penetrating into the south. So there we find good architecture still being built, e. g. the temple of Subrahmaṇya at Tanjore, one of the finest examples of the Dravidian style in existence. In the sixteenth and seventeenth centuries the greater temples were enclosed with enormous walls and were frequently used as forts. The gopurams of this period are of enormous height, but their sculpture is of stucco, and the style is everywhere flamboyant and decadent.

88. The religious movements of the north during these centuries fall into three groups, Rāmaite, Kṛishṇaite, and deistic; yet all the sects have a great many points in common, inherited from earlier forms of Vaishṇavism. They believe in one personal God who is full of love and pity for those who worship Him; yet all, except the followers of Kabīr, recognize the other gods, and worship idols; they all hold that the human soul is a portion of the Divine, and that it will eternally retain its individuality; they offer salvation to men of all castes, demanding faith and *bhakti* toward the Lord; they use the vernaculars instead of Sanskrit; they exalt the *guru*, the religious teacher, to a place of great authority; they use a *mantra*, i.e. a secret phrase or password, which is whispered by the guru to the novice on initiation; they partake of a sacramental meal; and each sect has its own order of ascetics as well as its congregation of the laity.

36. GOPURAM AT KUMBAKOṆAM
Photograph by Wiele and Klein.)

89. Of the Rāmaite leaders we shall mention the three most notable. Rāmānanda was a native of South India and was a leader in the Śrīsampradāya, the church of Rāmānuja; but in consequence of a quarrel he left the sect and migrated to North India. He gave up all the exclusiveness of Rāmānuja, and also his troublesome restrictions about food. He preached in Hindī, and admitted all castes, even the lowest, to his fold. 'He had twelve apostles, among whom were a Rājput, a currier, a barber, and a Muḥammadan weaver.' The whole *bhakti* movement in the north owes a great debt to Rāmānanda. He belongs to the first half of the fifteenth century; yet his theology and practice show no trace of Muḥammadan influence.

37. FLAMBOYANT PILLARS IN DRAVIDIAN TEMPLE

Tulsī Dās belonged to the church of Rāmānanda. His activity was contemporaneous with the reign of the great Akbar and of his son Jahāngīr. He alone among the *bhakti* leaders did not found a sect. He preferred to influence all his fellow-countrymen; and he has won his reward; for the millions of the people of Upper India to-day acknowledge Tulsī Dās as their guide. The teaching which he imparted as he wandered over the land he gave permanent form to in the *Rāmacharit Mānas*, 'the Lake of the deeds of Rama'. It is a modern Rāmāyaṇa in the sense that it recounts the old story, but it is shot through and through with *bhakti* theology and with the healthy moral spirit of the poet. The language is Eastern Hindī. Those who know say that he produced 'some of the most beautiful poetry which has found birth in Asia'; and the common people of the north show by their devotion to his great work that they agree with this high praise.

Nābhā Dās, a contemporary of Tulsī Dās, wrote the *Bhakta Mālā*, or 'Garland of Devotees', a series of brief biographies of the chief *bhakti* saints.

90. The Kṛishṇaite books in Sanskrit noticed in our last chapter were followed up by some very interesting vernacular literature in the latter half of the fifteenth century. Vidyāpati wrote many lyrics in the dialect of Bihār; Chaṇḍī Dās did similar work in Bengali; and in Rājputāna, Mīrā Bāī, a princess, wrote beautiful songs, which are extremely popular, in the Braj Bhāshā. This is the dialect of the country round Mathurā, where Kṛishṇa's life among the cowherds is fabled to have been lived. In this very country the first fully systematized form of popular Kṛishṇaism was founded in the early part of the sixteenth century by a Brāhman from the south named Vallabhāchārya. In his teaching and among his followers the sensual and sexual elements which are present in all the later Kṛishṇaite mythology come to the front and bear their evil harvest. His son-in-law Chaitanya preached the faith of Kṛishṇa in Bengal, using the lyrics of Vidyāpati to stir the emotions of the people. He was essentially a revivalist appealing to the feelings by music, singing, and devotional excitement. In his own time the nobler elements of the religion were in the ascendant; but soon immorality crept in and degraded the movement seriously. The most famous of Vallabhāchārya's successors was Sūr Dās, the blind poet of Agra. His work is called the *Sūr-Sāgar*, and consists of exquisite songs on the legend of Kṛishṇa in the Braj dialect. Nāmdev and Tukārām, who were both Marāṭhās, were Kṛishṇaites. Tukārām's poems are greatly treasured.

All the modern *Bhāgavatas* reckon themselves to belong

to one or other of four Mother-churches, though there are numerous subdivisions.

Though both Rāmaites and Kṛishṇaites accepted men of every caste as members of their sects, yet they never dreamed of doing away with caste. (See section 64.)

91. The deistic movement springs from Kabīr, the Muḥammadan weaver who was one of the apostles of Rāmānanda. Here Muḥammadan influence makes itself distinctly felt. For, though Kabīr was a disciple of Rāmānanda, though he calls God by the name Rāma, and has Vedāntic ideas, he will have nothing to do with the doctrine of incarnations, and he condemns idolatry and caste with unsparing voice. Yet he is recognized as an incarnation himself by his followers, the Kabīrpanthīs; and his polemic against caste has had but little effect: the Hindu and the Muḥammadan members of his Church have separate monasteries and have little in common except their devotion to their Master; and the Hindu members are almost all Śūdras. His pithy couplets and epigrammatic sayings are still very popular. Dādū, a sixteenth-century cotton-cleaner of Ahmadābād, leader of the Dādūpanthīs, got his theology from Kabīr.

No direct influence exerted by Kabīr, however, is equal to the indirect influence which has arisen through the founding of the Sikh sect in the Punjab by his disciple Nānak. From the beginning the chief guru of the church exercised large power; and the tenth guru, named Govind, took such steps as transformed the sect into a military order and finally created a great and warlike nation. But no guru succeeded Govind, and their sacred book, the *Granth*, is now the centre of the faith. It is a most interesting collection of varied material, some of it very trivial, some very valuable. Much of it was written by the gurus, but there are also hymns and sayings from all the great *bhakti* teachers of the north. The most important part, the *Ādi Granth* or 'Original

Book', was compiled by Guru Arjun in 1601. Govind Singh added a great deal of new matter in 1696, and the whole is now called the *Granth.* Nānak condemned idolatry, and Guru Govind abolished caste within the military order. Yet caste is now rife among the Sikhs; and the *Granth* is treated like an idol in their central shrine, the Golden Temple of Amṛitsar.

It is a most extraordinary fact that the theology of Kabīr was meant to unite Hindus and Muḥammadans in the worship of the one God; yet the most implacable hatred arose between the Sikhs and the Muḥammadans; and from that hatred came the Khālsā, the Sikh military order, which created the fiercest enemies the Mughal emperors had. It is also most noteworthy that caste has found its way back into every Hindu sect that has disowned it. (See section 81.)

92. In the fourteenth century a new Vishṇuite movement appeared at Udipi, in the Canarese country. The founder of the church is known as Madhvāchārya, his followers as Śrīmādhvas. Madhva was a sannyāsī, and, like the other āchāryas, he made his reputation by a commentary on the *Vedānta-sūtras.* His system is a dualism, and is frankly called *dvaita*, dualistic. If Rāmānuja is farther from Śaṅkara than Nīlakaṇṭha, Madhva is still more distant. The sect of the Śrīmādhvas has attained considerable proportions and influence, especially in Western India. Later leaders produced hymns in Canarese; so that there is an opportunity for popularizing the doctrine. But Madhva was much more exclusive than either the Śaivas or the followers of Rāmānuja. He laid great stress on caste, on cleanliness of person and clothes, and on temple ritual. Kṛishṇa was his favourite divinity.

In the thirteenth and fourteenth centuries the Śaivas of the south developed their teaching into a philosophical system which is called the *Śaiva Siddhānta*, and which is expressed in a series of Tamil books, partly in verse, partly in prose. The teachers who produced this vernacular literature receive the title āchārya.

93. Muḥammadan influence touched Hindus effectively in another direction. Partly in self-defence, partly in imitation of their masters, the upper classes of Hindu society began to seclude their women: the zenāna system dates from Muḥammadan times. Like other high-class customs, it is copied by the lower classes so far as their means will allow.

NOTE.—The text below is by Nānak, and is from the daily liturgy of the Sikhs in the *Ādi Granth*. The language is Hindī, but the script is Gurmukhī:—

'In the beginning was the Real, in the beginning of the ages was the Real. The Real, O Nānak, is, and the Real also will be.'

ਆਦਿ ਸਚੁ ਜੁਗਾਦਿ ਸਚੁ ॥

ਹੈ ਭੀ ਸਚੁ ਨਾਨਕ ਹੋਸੀ ਭੀ ਸਚੁ ॥

ILLUSTRATIVE READINGS

24. Baby Rāma in His Mother's Arms

With fingers locked in prayer she cries,—'How may I dare,
O lord god immortal, thy boundless praise to tell?—
Far above the world's confusion and reason's vain intrusion, whom all the scriptures witness incomprehensible;
Whom saints and holy sages have hymned through all the ages, the fountain of compassion, the source of every grace;
Who aye with Lakshmī reignest, thou, even thou, now deignest to be my son and succour thy sore-tried chosen race.
Though we know by revelation, heaven and earth and all creation, in each hair upon thy body may be found,
In my arms thou sweetly dreamest, O mystery supremest, far beyond the comprehension of a sage the most profound.'
Smiled the lord at her devotion, and would fain have set in motion the magic that dazzles the crowd,
Telling all he had done and the triumphs he had won, that his mother of her son might be proud.
But hurriedly she cried,—'My soul is terrified by these marvels, disperse them from my sight;
Let me see thee as a child, disporting free and wild, for in this is my greatest delight.'
She spoke and he obeyed, and, at once in fashion made, as an infant began to cry.

Tulsī Dās, *Rāmacharit Mānas*, Book I, Chhand, 24–7; Growse's Translation, pp. 96–7.

25. The Praise of Kṛishṇa in Marāṭhī

(a) *Kṛishṇa's Saving Power*

What or whom shall we ask for but thee, O thou who fillest the globe and the universe? Who else knows how to fulfil our heart's desires? What of other princes and kings? There is none other in the three worlds that grants liberation, none that saves us but thou. When we think upon thy name and form, sin and fever run away in fear, desire is destroyed. Hari, this name of thine is truly called such in the Purāṇas, for it drives away death and re-incarnation from those they have seized. Why should I waste my speech? It is fruitless for me to praise any other than thee. O thou that destroyest the world, the great serpent is wearied with describing thee. Let my spirit repose in confidence at thy feet; it is vain to ask for aught else. Thy title, 'Lord of the humble', is justified in the eyes of men; thou hast saved many a humble, many a guilty, many a sinful man. Tukā dwells at thy feet; preserve him, O God! I ask that I may serve thee.

(b) *Tukārām's Religious Experience*

Step by step he supports me: my life is led on to perfection. I have found an assured place in him, and the world I have left void. My spirit goes forward on the path. I am filled in the flesh with growing joy. Tukā says, In this mortal world I have joined the pervading spirit.

The Poems of Tukārām, Fraser and Marathe, pp. 89 and 245.

TABLES

23. The Bhakti Period, 1200 to 1757

External Events	*History*	*Religion*	*Literature*
1200		The Qutb Minār and Mosque built	Nāmdev Mey-kaṇḍa-devar
1300	1336 Vijayanagar founded 1398 Taimūr in India		Umāpati Madhva Sāyaṇa and Mādhava
1400			Vidyāpati Rāmānanda Mīrā Bāī Kabīr
1500 Martin Luther	1526 the Mughals		Nānak
	1556 Akbar	Toleration	
1588 The Armada	1565 Battle of Tālikoṭ. Fall of Vijayanagar		Sūr Dās Tulsī Dās Dādū
			Chaitanya *Bhakta Mālā*
1600		Intolerance renewed	1601 *Ādi Granth*
Cromwell	1658 Aurungzeb		Tukārām
			1696 *Granth*

24. The Tamil Literature of the Śaiva Siddhānta

A. The twelve canonical books, called *Tirumurai* or *Drāviḍa Śruti*:—

Cent.	*Authors*	*Books*	
VII	Appar	The *Devāram*	3
	Ñāna Sambandhar		3
VIII	Sundarar		1
X	Māṇikka Vāchakar	*Tiruvāchakam* and *Tirukovaiyār*	1
	Nine authors:	*Tiruviśaipā*	1
	Tirumūlar:	*Tirumantram*	1
	Nambi-āṇḍār-nambi:		1
	Śekkiḻār:	*Periya Purāṇam*	1
			12

B. The fourteen *Siddhānta Śāstras*. Of these the most important are:—

XIII	Mey-kaṇḍa-devar	*Śiva-ñāna-bodham*, a systematic statement of the principles of the faith, translated from the *Raurava Āgama*
	Mana-vāchakam Kaḍandār	*Uṇmai Viḷakkam*
	Aruṇandi-devar	*Śiva-ñāna-siddhi*, a further exposition
XIV	Umāpati Śivāchāryar	*Śiva Prakāśam*, a poem in a hundred quatrains, being a commentary on the two preceding works
		Tiru-aruḷ-payan, a poem in a hundred couplets on divine grace

25. The Literature of the Śaivas and the Vaishṇavas

NOTE.—This table is meant to give some idea of the strikingly parallel development which these sects have had in South India. Both acknowledge the Vedas, though there are certain sections of them which they hold in less honour than their own literature. Both sects acknowledge to the full the inspiration and authority of the *Vedānta-sūtras.*

The following are the chief divisions of their respective literatures :—

	Śaivas	*Vaishṇavas*
1. Basal works in Sanskrit verse, taking the place of the Śrauta-sūtras and the Karma-mīmāṁsā	The Āgamas or Śaivāgamas	The Saṁhitās or Pāñcharātra Saṁhitās
2. Tamil Hymns by early saints	The *Devāram* of the three Adiyārs and Māṇikka Vāchakar's works	The *Nālāyira Prabandham* of the Aḷvārs
3. Commentary in Sanskrit prose on the *Vedānta-sūtras*	The *Śaiva Bhāshya* of Nīlakaṇṭha	The *Śrī Bhāshya* of Rāmānuja
4. Philosophic works in Tamil	The fourteen Siddhānta Śāstras	The *Artha Pañchaka* of Piḷḷai Lokāchārya and other books

26. The Followers of Rāmānanda

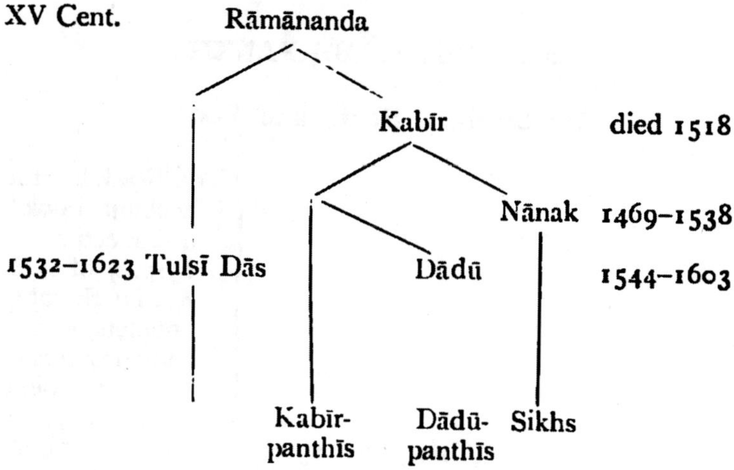

27. Adoration Mantras

(*a*) Bhāgavata :—

Oṁ namo Bhagavate Vāsudevāya, 'Om ! reverence to the adorable Vāsudeva.'

(*b*) Early Buddhist :—

Oṁ namo Bhagavate, 'Om ! reverence to the Adorable.'

(*c*) Later Buddhist :—

Namo 'mitābhāya, 'Reverence to Amitābha.'

(*d*) The five syllables of the Śaiva Siddhānta, *Śivāya namaḥ*, 'Reverence to Śiva.'

(*e*) The followers of Rāmānuja :—

Oṁ namo Nārāyaṇāya, 'Om ! reverence to Nārāyaṇa.'

(*f*) The followers of Rāmānanda :—

Oṁ Rāmāya namaḥ, 'Om ! reverence to Rāma.'

(*g*) The Vallabhāchārīs :—

Śrī Kṛishṇaḥ śaraṇaṁ mama, 'Holy Kṛishṇa is my refuge.'

28. THE KABĪRPANTH

Its Leaders, Sects and Books

KABĪR, died 1518

The *Bījak*, lit. 'the account-book', a collection of hymns, of *Sākhīs*, i.e. rhyming couplets, and of short prose expositions of points of doctrine, published about 1570. Many of these re-appear in the *Ādi Granth*. Multitudes of other *Sākhīs* are current and are attributed to Kabīr.

The *Bāp*, i.e. Father, section at the Kabīr Chaura, Benares, and at Maghār, Gorakhpur District, where Kabīr died.
Founder:
SURAT GOPĀL.

The *Mai*, i.e. Mother, section at Chatisgarh, C.P.
Founder:
DHARM DĀS

Sukh Nidān, a manual of doctrine published in 1729.
Amar Mūl, another manual of later origin.

29. Canon of the Vedānta, the Prasthānatraya

A. The Upanishads. The following eleven are usually studied: *Chhāndogya*, *Kena*, *Aitareya*, *Kaushītaki*, *Īśā*, *Kāṭhaka*, *Muṇḍaka*, *Taittirīya*, *Bṛihadāraṇyaka*, *Śvetāśvatara*, *Praśna*.

B. The Bhagavadgītā.

C. The Vedānta-sūtras.

Note.—In studying these sacred books the *Advaitī* follows Śaṅkara, the *Viśishṭādvaitī* follows Rāmānuja, the *Dvaiti* follows Madhva, and the Śaivite sects follow Nīlakaṇṭha.

38. Picture from Kabīr Chaura Monastery, Benares

Surat Gopāl and Dharm Dās kneel in front of Kabīr, while his son Kamāl fans him. (Photograph kindly favoured by the Bishop of Lucknow.)

30. Northern Kṛishṇaite Leaders

Century	*Name*	*Place*	*Works*	*Language*
XI	Nimbārka	......	......	......
XII	Jayadeva	Bengal	*Gītā Govinda*	Sanskrit
XIII	Nāmdev	Marāṭhā Land	Hymns	Marāṭhī
XIV	......	......	... .	......
XV	Vidyāpati Chaṇḍī Dās Mīrā Bāī	Bihār Bengal Mewāṛ	Sonnets Songs Songs	Maithilī Bengali Braj
XVI	Vallabha Sūr Dās Chaitanya	Mathura Agra Nadīya	*Sūr Sāgar*	Braj Bengali
XVII	Tukārām	Marāṭhā Land	*Abhaṅgs*, hymns	Marāṭhī

31. The Modern Bhāgavatas

	The Four Churches	*Philosophic Position*	*Main Sect*	*Chief Sub-sects*
RĀMAITE	I. ŚRĪ-SAMPRADĀYA Founder: RĀMĀNUJA	*Viśishṭādvaita*, Modified monism	Śrī-sampradāyas	1. Rāmānandīs 2. Kabīrpanthīs 3. Khākīs 4. Mulūk-dāsīs 5. Rai-dāsīs 6. Senā-panthīs
RĀMAITE	II. BRAHMA-SAMPRADĀYA Founder: MADHVA	*Dvaita*, Dualism	Mādhvas	
KṚISHṆAITE	III. RUDRA-SAMPRADĀYA Founder: VISHṆU-SVĀMI	*Śuddhādvaita*, Pure monism	Vallabhā-chārīs	1. Mīrā Bāīs 2. Chaitanyas
KṚISHṆAITE	IV. SANAKĀDI-SAMPRADĀYA Founder: NIMBĀRKA	*Dvaitādvaita*, Dualistic monism	Nimāvats	1. Rādhā-Valla-bhas 2. Charaṇ-dāsīs 3. Sakhi-bhāvas

NOTE.—Sampradāya means tradition. Thus Śrī-sampradāya means the tradition handed down from Śrī, i. e. Lakshmī, the wife of Vishṇu. The second tradition is said to come from Brahmā, the Creator, the third from Rudra, i. e. Śiva, and the fourth from the sage Sanaka and his brethren.

পূর্ব্বে কেবল এক পরব্রহ্ম মাত্র ছিলেন; অন্য আর কিছুই ছিল না; তিনি এই সমুদয় সৃষ্টি করিলেন।

CHAPTER XI

PERIOD OF WESTERN INFLUENCE

PROTESTANT MISSIONS: REVIVAL OF HINDUISM

From the Battle of Plassey onward: A.D. 1757–1910

94. *History.* It is extremely difficult to give any satisfactory account of the fragment of a period with which we deal in this chapter. The great forces which are at work have only begun to evolve the results with which they are pregnant; so that the writer has to choose between a recital of facts without any attempt at appraisement and an estimate of their meaning which must of necessity be largely of the nature of a prophecy. Yet it is so important to give the student of Hinduism some idea of the forces set in motion during the nineteenth century that the attempt must be made at all costs.

Violence and confusion continued long after the battle of Plassey; so that Western influence scarcely made itself felt in the life of the people until the dawn of the nineteenth century. Since then the whole political history of India is summed up in the gradual extension and consolidation of the British power and in its progressive adaptation to the needs of the people. The Mutiny and the recent outburst

Note.—The above text is the first of the four clauses of the *Bīja*, 'seed', of Brāhma doctrine drawn up by Devendra Nāth Tagore: 'In the beginning there was only one supreme Brahman; there was nothing else; He created all this.' The language is Bengali.

of anarchism were but tragic episodes, and scarcely exercised any positive influence on the real movement of the time. Yet, though the period under review is very short, in no preceding period have such revolutionary changes been produced on the Indian mind. The only time in any way comparable with the present is that which we dealt with in our fourth chapter, when Essential Hinduism arose; but that was a normal development compared with the upheaval we see around us to-day.

Western influence is an atmosphere, a new climate, which has found its way into Indian life, and it acts as imperceptibly, as powerfully, and as universally as the atmosphere. Yet the channels through which this impalpable element has been brought into the environment of all Indians may be distinguished.

(*a*) The most important of these is *Western education*, whether given in school or college, in the vernacular or English, by Government teacher, missionary, Hindu or Theosophist.

(*b*) The second place is held by *Christian teaching*, whether oral or literary. Both the direct presentation of Christian ideas, religious, moral, and social, and the less welcome criticism of Hinduism, have been of incalculable service.

(*c*) In the third rank stands *Christian philanthropy*, whether carried on by missionary societies or by Government agencies. All that has been done for the sick, the famine-stricken, for orphans and lepers, for the ignorant and the downtrodden, has been potent to wake the conscience of India. The earnest efforts of the Government to rule for the good of the people, to treat all races, religions, and castes as equal, and to give every one strict justice, has been an object-lesson of the utmost power.

(*d*) The brilliant work done by *Western scholars* on

ancient Indian literature has, on the one hand, opened the eyes of Hindus to the real history of India and of their religion in contrast with the old traditions, but, on the other hand, has filled them with a new pride in their religion and has given thousands courage to remain within the Hindu fold.

These forms of activity have created a new race of men, the educated classes; and through them to-day India is being rejuvenated. Around us on every side the new life is pulsing, expanding, remaking the country. The railway, the post office, the telegraph, the steamer, and European manufactures and commerce, have touched the masses of India in some degree, but it is through the educated men that the new age is being inaugurated. They are marked by their English speech, by great enthusiasm for education, a passion for self-government, a desire for economic progress, a new attitude to women, fresh humanitarian feeling, and a consciousness that the new India of their dreams cannot be brought in without many reforms. All this is summed up to-day under the phrase 'the National Movement'.

95. *Religion.* Hindus frequently declare that Hinduism, largely as a result of many decades of devastation and chaos, had fallen very low indeed by the opening of the nineteenth century. There can be no doubt of the truth of this statement. Scholarship was seriously contracted; spirituality remained only in the quiet places of the land; a coarse ritualism was supreme in all the great centres of population; and the more repulsive features of the religion, such as gross idolatry, immorality, infanticide, *satī*, hook-swinging, and other tortures, were very much in evidence. Unless this is understood, the course of events during the century is not comprehensible.

During our period there has been no internal development of Hinduism whatsoever. All that has to be chronicled is the results produced on Hinduism and the Hindus by Western influence.

The period under review falls very naturally into three subdivisions, 1800–30, 1830–75, 1875–1910.

A. During the thirty years between 1800–30 the two most potent sources of influence upon the Hindu mind were, without doubt, the British Government and the Serampore missionaries.

During those thirty years the idea that Britain was responsible for the welfare of India was first distinctly recognized; and the new spirit made itself manifest in a number of ways. The College of Fort William, Calcutta, was founded by Lord Wellesley to give Indian civilians a real knowledge of the people they were to govern. While the empire was steadily expanded, methods of government were as steadily improved, and new conceptions of policy took form. In 1826 began the great crusade against *thagī*, i. e. the system of strangling and robbing wealthy travellers; in 1829 Bentinck put down *satī*; and about the same time the long-continued crusade against female infanticide was begun.

The great triad, Carey, Marshman, and Ward, however, did far more to wake the Indian intellect than the Government of India. The actual baptism of Brāhman converts was an unspeakable shock: what else could have so effectually roused the Hindu? By literature more than by speech the missionaries started the effective diffusion of Christian teaching in North India; they scattered the Bible broadcast over the peninsula in the vernaculars; they began the printing of Indian literature in both Sanskrit and the vernaculars; they began the use of Bengali prose, and published the first vernacular newspaper; they were the pioneers of widespread education; and lastly, their bold exposure of the cruelties and immoralities of customary Hinduism, though crude and harsh to us to-day, was absolutely necessary to wake Hindus to a consciousness of the glaring faults of their religion.

Apart from the foundation of the Christian Church of

Bengal, the one noticeable religious outcome of these thirty years is the life and work of Rāja Rām Mohan Rai, who set a fine example in his study of Hinduism ; who stood by the missionaries in their attack on *satī* and other cruelties ; and who founded the Brāhma Samāj. His influence has been continuously felt down to our own days.

B. Since Duff's work colours all the religious history of the middle of the nineteenth century, we begin our second subdivision, 1830–75, with the year of his arrival in Calcutta.

In 1834 the Government of India, largely under Duff's influence, decided to favour Western instead of Oriental education. Henceforward both Government and the missionary societies pressed forward the foundation of High Schools and Colleges. The Universities of Calcutta, Bombay, and Madras were founded in 1857 amid the throes of the Mutiny. Government continued to put down immoral abuses in Hinduism and Indian life.

During these decades Protestant Missions in India developed several new methods, and laid firmly the foundations of their future work. Apart from the Higher Education, which as a missionary method was largely the fruit of Duff's genius, the chief new creations were work by women for women and medical Missions.

The Brāhma Samāj is a Unitarian reforming movement, which arose within Hinduism under Rām Mohan Rai, but renounced caste and other Hindu forms of life during this subdivision of our period under Devendra Nāth Tagore and Keshab Chandra Sen. The movement is strictly theistic and strongly opposed to idolatry. Its moral ideas and forms of worship are practically Christian.

By far the most powerful religious influences during those years were missionary effort, especially as exerted through High Schools and Colleges, and the Brāhma Samāj. The

Protestant Church of India had its foundation laid strong and deep through the accession of groups of students won from the heart of Hinduism by Duff and other educational missionaries. Another stream of awakened men passed into the Brāhma Samāj, chiefly in Bengal, but to some extent also in Bombay, Madras, and Lahore. Yet, sad to say, in Bengal at least, a far larger number of young men became atheists or agnostics, and led a rather reckless social revolt against the restrictions of Hinduism. The new illumination did not by any means lead to spiritual results in all cases.

C. About 1875 a remarkable change makes itself manifest in the Indian spirit. Until then it seemed to have been at school. Now it seems to reach maturity and begins to act with all the vivacity and spontaneity of youth. An extraordinary number of fresh movements, educational, political, religious, social, economic, have arisen all over the country. Educated men are everywhere alive, filled with excitement, ambition, new capacities, new activities. We choose 1875 as the dividing line, because in that year both the Ārya Samāj and the Theosophical Society were founded.

Government has increasingly given itself to the effort to better the material and moral well-being of the people, especially by means of education, irrigation, railways, and famine-relief, but has been compelled to adopt a cautious policy towards the political aspirations of the educated, and thus has seemed on the surface to be more critical than sympathetic towards the National Movement.

Missions during these years have exercised a powerful influence through the conversion of vast masses of the depressed classes, who throughout the centuries have been considered too unclean for contact with pure Hindus. (See sections 45 and 120.) Largely through these mass movements the Protestant Church in India has increased in numbers much more rapidly than any other religious body.

The great feature of these decades, however, is the revival of Hinduism. As a result of the attack of Protestant Christianity, on the one hand, and of the rise of interest in Oriental religions in the West, on the other hand, Hindus have been roused to a great rally in defence of their ancestral faith. Every one will remember the parallel revival of the pagan faiths of the Roman Empire in the second and following centuries. The revival is found wherever there are educated Hindus, and it has taken many forms, but four organizations stand out above all others as leading the movement.

(*a*) The first of these is the Ārya Samāj, founded by Dayānanda Sarasvatī in the Punjab. It is strictly theistic and denounces idolatry. The founder also denounced caste, but the members of the Samāj do not practise what he preached: they remain within Hinduism. The Vedas are the only sacred book acknowledged; and even portions of them are not accepted as inspired. The Samāj is vehemently anti-Christian, and has shown strong political leanings. It has grown very rapidly during the last twenty years, but only in the Punjab and the United Provinces.

(*b*) The second organization is the Theosophical Society, which was founded by Madame Blavatsky and Colonel Olcott in New York in 1875, but removed its head-quarters to India in 1878. It has three aims:

1. The formation of a real brotherhood amongst men of all nations and religions.

2. The study of Aryan, and especially of Oriental, religions.

3. The investigation of the occult powers of man.

Madame Blavatsky pretended to have intercourse with certain supernatural beings called Mahātmas, and all sorts of wonders were performed at the head-quarters in Madras. But the trickery was exposed, and Madame Blavatsky fled from India, never to return.

The Society, however, has continued to grow and flourish in India, first under Colonel Olcott, and then under Mrs. Besant. The position maintained is that every religion is legitimate and right, and that anything like proselytism is to be condemned. Yet Theosophy teaches Karma and Transmigration, and thus proclaims itself a friend to Hinduism and Buddhism and alien to all other faiths. It has been vehemently anti-Christian throughout its history in India. There can be no question that it has gained its position in India because it has defended Hindu idols and caste as well as philosophy. It came just at the moment when the Hindu wanted a champion, and multitudes of Hindus to-day feel safe behind its sophistries. The Society has done considerable service to India in the matter of education. Like the Islāmia College at Aligarh, the Central Hindu College at Benares is modelled on missionary lines. In all earlier Hindu colleges for Western education no religious training was given, but in Benares Hinduism is taught, as Muḥammadanism is taught at Aligarh.

(*c*) The third organization sprang from an interesting ascetic named Rāmakṛishṇa Paramahaṁsa, who lived in a temple near Calcutta. He had had no serious education either Hindu or Western, but was full of mother-wit and practical common sense. Gauging well the tendencies of the time, he took up the old Hindu proverb, that as all rivers run to the sea, so all forms of Hinduism lead to salvation, and applied it to all the religions of the world. He was ready to accept and to practise any aspect of Hinduism, and he imagined himself now a Christian, now a Muḥammadan. He gathered a band of disciples around him and exercised considerable influence over the Brāhma leader, Keshab Chandra Sen. By far the greatest of his disciples was Svāmī Vivekānanda, who spoke at the Chicago Parliament of Religions, and then lectured with great success all over India. He sent out missionaries to Britain and to America; and, before his early death, founded several monasteries in India in which work still continues. He and his followers defend the whole of Hinduism.

(*d*) By 1890 these three movements had stirred the educated classes of India very deeply, and there arose a whole army of lecturers, monks, and teachers, who went from town to town, delivering apologetic lectures, expounding the sacred books, holding classes for their study, and founding societies for the defence of Hinduism. Out of these there sprang the fourth organization, the most orthodox of all, the Bhārat Dharma Mahāmandal, under the leadership of the Mahārāja of Darbhaṅga, branches of which have been formed far and wide and have proved very influential.

The Brāhma Samāj has continued to work steadily throughout the years, but since the death of Keshab in 1884 it has had much less influence. The Prārthanā Samāj, which arose in the Bombay presidency in 1867, as a result of the work of the Brāhma Samāj, was long led by a very remarkable man, Mr. Justice Ranade. The main difference between the two is this, that full membership in the Brāhma Samāj places a man outside Hindu society, while members of the Prārthanā Samāj continue in the old religion. From the Prārthanā Samāj and Mr. Justice Ranade there sprang the Social Reform Movement, which has gradually attained influence all over the country and is a most healthy leaven. Its organ is the *Indian Social Reformer*.

With the smaller movements we cannot deal in detail. Each of the sects has now its defence association and annual conference.

All the organizations have a great deal in common. To be thoroughly Hindu, and at the same time to introduce just as much reform as is necessary to make the religion practically efficient in these modern days, and so to prove that Christianity is unnecessary—this is the ideal. Each section opposes Christianity; yet each copies missionary methods down to the last detail, and endeavours to prove that its theology is as strictly monotheistic as Christianity and its morality as lofty and practical.

It is most noteworthy that movements in all essentials similar to the revival of Hinduism have taken place among the Jains, the Parsees, and the Muḥammadans of India, and amongst the Buddhists of Burma and Ceylon, not to mention China and Japan.

96. *Literature*. The literature of our period cannot compare with that of earlier periods in value or in literary power, but its interest is very great.

The literature of the Brāhma Samāj is perhaps higher in quality than any other. Rāja Rām Mohan Rai published translations in English and Bengali of the leading Upanishads, but his most remarkable work was *The Precepts of Jesus*, being a catena of passages from the Gospels. Devendra Nāth Tagore prepared *Brāhma Dharma*, a volume of extracts from the Upanishads, meant to be used both as a service-book and as a manual of devotion. Keshab published a remarkable service-book called *Śloka Saṅgraha*, containing texts from Hindu, Buddhist, Sikh, Jewish, Christian, Muḥammadan, Parsee, and Chinese Scriptures. His volumes of lectures are interesting and illuminating. The only other work of genius written by a Brāhma is Mozoomdar's *Oriental Christ*.

The founder of the Ārya Samāj was no modern scholar, and so his works on the Hindu Scriptures are of no value, but, for the theology and organization of the Samāj, his *Satyārtha Prakāśa* is of great importance. Rāmakṛishṇa Paramahaṁsa left nothing written, but Max Müller published a volume containing a brief account of his life and a large number of his sayings as reported by disciples. Svāmī Vivekānanda's writings show a manly independence and a national spirit which are altogether admirable, but they are marred by distortion of history and extreme exaggeration. Theosophy has produced a large literature, and Mrs. Besant has published many works on Hinduism, some of which one must read in order to understand her influence. Mr. Justice Ranade's writings are full of ethical and intellectual force.

A vast Hindu literature has kept falling from the Indian press in all the chief cities during the last thirty years, editions of the sacred books, above all of the *Gītā*, commentaries and translations both in English and the vernaculars, and defences of the teaching of the various Hindu sects. The earliest and most noteworthy of this latter group is probably the Neo-Kṛishṇa literature of Bengal, the leading writer being Bankim Chandra Chatterji. The protagonist of the Vaishṇavism of South India is Mr. Govindāchārya Svāmī of Mysore; of the Śaiva-Siddhānta, Mr. Nallasvāmī Piḷḷai; and of Mādhvism, Mr. Padmanābhāchār of Coimbatore; while Mr. Sundararāman of Kumbakoṇam stands almost alone as the defender of the whole of ancient ritualistic Hinduism.

NOTE.—The text below in Bengali is by Rāmakṛishṇa Paramahaṁsa. 'As some people come to this House of Kālī by boat, some by carriage and some on foot—various people by various means at last reaching the same spot; so, though men are various and their creeds are various, yet the God whom they find by them is in all cases the same.'

যেমন এই কালীবাটিতে আসিতে হইলে কেহ নৌকায় কেহ গাড়িতে এবং কেহ হাঁটিয়া আসিয়া থাকে। ভিন্ন ২ উপায়ে ভিন্ন ২ ব্যক্তি পরিশেষে একস্থানে আসিয়া উপস্থিত হয়। সেইরূপ ভিন্ন ২ ব্যক্তির ভিন্ন ২ মতের দ্বারা যে ঈশ্বর লাভ হইয়া থাকে তাহা সকলেরই এক॥

ILLUSTRATIVE READINGS

26. The Folly of Idolatry

NOTE.—This is a passage from the autobiography of Dayānanda Sarasvatī. It refers to a time in his boyhood, when his father insisted on initiating him into the worship of Śiva.

As a preparation for this solemn act I was made to fast, and I had then to follow my father for a night's vigil in the temple of Śiva. The vigil is divided into four parts or praharas, consisting of three hours each. When I had watched six hours I observed about midnight that the Pūjāris, the temple-servants, and some of the devotees, after having left the inner temple, had fallen asleep. Knowing that this would destroy all the good effects of the service, I kept awake myself, when I observed that even my father had fallen asleep. While I was thus left alone I began to meditate. Is it possible, I asked myself, that this idol I see bestriding his bull before me, and who, according to all accounts, walks about, eats, sleeps, drinks, holds a trident in his hand, beats the drum, and can pronounce curses on men, can be the great Deity, the Mahādeva, the Supreme Being? Unable to resist such thoughts any longer I roused my father, asking him to tell me whether this hideous idol was the great god of the scriptures. 'Why do you ask?' said my father. 'Because', I answered, 'I feel it impossible to reconcile the idea of an omnipotent living God with this idol, which allows the mice to run over his body and thus suffers himself to be polluted without the slightest protest.'

Max Müller, *Biographical Essays*, p. 172 f.

27. A New Reading of History

Before even the Buddhists were born, there are evidences accumulating every day that Indian thought penetrated the world. Vedanta, before Buddhism, had penetrated into China, into Persia, and the Islands of the Eastern Archipelago. Again, when the mighty mind of the Greek had linked the different parts of the eastern world together, there came Indian thought; and Christianity with all its boasted civilization is a collection of little bits of Indian thought. Ours is the religion of which Buddhism, with all its greatness, is the rebel child and Christianity a very patchy imitation. One of these cycles has again arrived. There is the tremendous power of England which has linked the different parts of the world together. English roads no more are content like Roman roads to run over lands, but they have ploughed the deep in every one of its parts. From ocean to ocean run the roads of England. Every part of the world has been linked to every other part, and electricity plays a most marvellous part as the new messenger. Under all these circumstances we find again India reviving and ready to give her own quota for the progress and civilization of the world. . . . Everything looks propitious, and Indian thought, philosophical and spiritual, must once more go over and conquer the world. . . . I am an imaginative man, and my idea is the conquest of the whole world by the Hindu race. . . . Up, India, and conquer the world with your spirituality! . . . The world wants it; without it the world will be destroyed. The whole of the western world is on a volcano which may burst to-morrow.

Svāmī Vivekānanda, *Madras Lectures*, pp. 83, 84, 85.

बर्हिषदः पितर ऊत्य१र्वागिमा वो हव्या चकृमा जुषध्वं ।
त आ गतावसा शंतमेनाथा नः शं योररपो दधात ॥

CHAPTER XII

OUTLINE OF THE HISTORY OF THE HINDU FAMILY

97. The beginnings of the Hindu family must be traced to the foundation of *the Patriarchal family* in prehistoric times on the basis of ancestor-worship. The natural results of this form of family organization are that the family and its morality are greatly strengthened; the father's authority is indefinitely enhanced; marriage becomes universal; the birth of a son is ardently desired; woman tends to be depreciated.

Girls were not welcomed so eagerly as boys; hence the custom of *the exposure of girl-babies* arose. This began in early prehistoric times.

The husband being the head of the family, a wife was regarded as one of his possessions, and *polygamy* therefore naturally arose. Hindu Mahārājas still exercise this ancient right; and any Hindu is free to marry a second wife, if the first prove barren. This also is prehistoric.

98. Gradual rise of the *Joint Family*. Each daughter goes to the home of her husband's father; but each son

NOTE.—The text at the top of the page refers to ANCESTOR-WORSHIP IN THE TIMES OF THE ṚIGVEDA:—

'Fathers, who sit on sacred grass, come, help us:
These offerings have we made for you, accept them.
So come to us with most auspicious favour,
And give us health and strength without a trouble.'

Ṛigveda, X. xv. 4.

brings his bride into his father's house. The granddaughters and grandsons do likewise. Hence there may be, and often are, four generations all living together in one house, under the control of the one father. In his hands are the earnings of all; and every member of the family is carefully looked after. The unity of the family is preserved, and the weaker members are cared for, but independence of character suffers.

When the Hindu patriarchal family began to develop, and the father became more and more important, the rule arose that *a man must not eat with his wife*. This regulation probably dates from the seventh or eighth century B.C.

99. It became the rule before the sixth century B.C. that every boy of the twice-born castes should be educated. This excellent rule fell into disuse long ago. Though every boy received an education, *no education was provided for a girl.*

100. By the fifth century B.C. it was the rule that a *girl must be married before puberty*. The natural consequence of this religious law was that parents, in their eagerness to secure a marriage for their daughters, betrothed them and had the marriage ceremony performed very early. Thus child-marriage became the Hindu custom. Hence through the death of boy-husbands, virgin child-widows of all ages, from a few months old, are common.

Only childless widows were allowed to remarry at this time.

101. Manu's Law-book ordains that *no widow, not even a virgin child-widow, may remarry*. The exact date of the book is unknown; but it is certain that this must have been the Hindu custom by the time of the birth of Christ.

102. The custom of *Satī*, widow-burning, came gradually into use in the early Christian centuries and was embodied in a code somewhere about the sixth century. The rule ran that only a widow who wished to become a *Satī* was allowed to mount the pyre; but it is certain that there were many unwilling victims. Rām Mohan Rai witnessed the burning of a widow who struggled to escape, his own brother's wife. It was only in North India that it became very common, and it was in Bengal that the largest number of cases occurred.

103. At the same time it became the rule that a widow who does not mount the pyre must spend her life in *perpetual mourning and asceticism*. In Bengal the rule is that a widow has to lay aside all her ornaments, wear a *sāri* without a border, subsist on a vegetarian diet, eat only one meal per day and twice a month pass a whole day of twenty-four hours without eating or drinking. In many parts of the country widows have to submit to tonsure. And on the top of all they are usually made household drudges. There are certain parts of the country where their lot is not quite so hard.

104. *The zenāna system*, or custom of secluding the women of the upper castes in the woman's apartments, arose during the Muḥammadan period, perhaps partly in imitation of Muslim custom, but mainly in self-defence. This practice does not affect in the same degree those provinces that came little under Muḥammadan domination. The zenāna is necessarily confined almost altogether to the upper castes. The women of the common people usually lead a very free life. Yet this custom, like other characteristics of high-caste life, is copied by the lower castes so far as their means will allow.

105. (*a*) Widow-burning prohibited by Lord Bentinck's Government, December 4, 1829.

(*b*) From 1830 onwards, a steady persistent crusade was carried on against female infanticide by the Government of India.

(*c*) In 1865 the Government passed a law legalizing the remarriage of Hindu widows.

NOTE.—The text below is on THE SUBJECTION OF WOMEN: 'Let her be in subjection to her father in her childhood, to her husband in her youth, to her sons when her husband is dead: let a woman never enjoy independence.' *Mānava Dharmaśāstra*, v. 148.

बाल्ये पितुर्वशे तिष्ठेत्पाणिग्राहस्य यौवने।
पुत्राणां भर्तरि प्रेते न भजेत्स्त्री स्वतन्त्रतां॥

अग्निहोत्रं समादाय गृह्यं चाग्निपरिच्छदम्।
ग्रामादरण्यं निःसृत्य निवसेन्नियतेन्द्रियः॥

CHAPTER XIII

OUTLINE OF THE HISTORY OF INDIAN ASCETICISM

106. In the Vedas and the Brāhmaṇas we meet with many references to *tapas*, austerity. Various forms of severe self-denial and self-torture were practised, such as the endurance of extreme cold or excessive heat, sustained fasts, the use of coarse and unnatural food, and such like. The belief was that by such means supernatural power could be obtained, or some definite desire fulfilled, or the highest place in heaven won, if only the pain were carried far enough. The ends being here material, not moral, this practice must be called ***materialistic austerity***.

107. Towards the end of the period of the Brāhmaṇas a new religious order appears. These men live in the forest and are therefore called *vānaprasthas*, i. e. forest-dwellers, hermits; and when a group of them live together, their retreat is called *āśrama*, hermitage. They keep up the worship of the gods by fire and prayer in the forests, and they practise the old *tapas*. It is still believed that by austerity many material blessings may be won; but the new idea, that by *tapas* the man may be purified and elevated

NOTE.—The text at the top of the page is THE RULE OF THE HERMIT, *Vānaprastha*: 'Carrying with him the sacred fire, and taking also the fire-utensils, he may go forth from the village to the forest and reside there with all his senses restrained.' *Mānava Dharmaśāstra*, vi. 4.

morally and spiritually, now appears; so that this is a new stage of thought and practice. We have here ***moral asceticism.*** The hermit retained his place in the family and in caste; he continued the worship of the gods and of his

39. TRIDAṆḌĪ ASCETIC

This is the high-priest of the Teṅ-galai (see section 81) Vishṇuites of the Tinnevelley District. Note the triple rod and the sect-mark, as in Rāmānuja's image (fig. 31). He wears a sacred thread, for, unlike the *Ekadaṇḍīs*, the *Tridaṇḍīs* do not give up caste. (Photographed for the author.)

ancestors; and he might even have his wife with him in his forest hut. He usually wore a coat of bark or of skin, lived usually on simple fare, and was forbidden to harm animals.

108. When the new Hindu theory of God and the world

arose—the one divine Reality behind all phenomena, the world worthless and unreal, transmigration and karma the only explanation of the sorrows and inequalities of the world—there came with it a great desire for Release from rebirth, and the belief that in order to win Release a man

40. Śivaite Sādhu with Head-dress

This extraordinary head-dress is in the form of a *liṅga*. He carries his *daṇḍa* in his right, his begging bowl in his left hand, wears a mass of necklaces of *rudraksha* berries and a cincture of bells. His face is smeared with ashes. (Photograph by Wiele & Klein.)

must give up the work, the interests, and the pleasures of men.

Consequently another religious order now appears, men who give up all their connexion with the life of man, relinquishing not only business and pleasure but wife and children, the worship of ancestors, the worship of the gods, property, house, ordinary food and clothing. They shaved off their hair, begged their food, and slept in a cave or at the root of a tree. Hence they were called *parivrājakas*, 'vagrants,' and *bhikshus*, 'beggars'. But the most significant name is *sannyāsīs*, 'renouncers,' because they renounced

41. SĀDHU WEARING SANDALS FILLED WITH SPIKES
(Photograph by Wiele & Klein.)

ordinary life so completely. The points to be noted are those that contrast with the hermit: worship is abandoned altogether; food and clothes are got by begging; and all connexion with the family, society, and the state is completely destroyed.

This new order of 'monks', as we shall call them, was

divided into numerous groups differing in faith and practice. Buddhist and Jain monks as well as all classes of Hindu monks had the same general ideal of the houseless life, as they called it. This form of discipline may be called *world-abandoning asceticism.*

109. Modern ascetics differ in several respects from the men of the earlier periods. The new ideas and practices came in with modern Hinduism. A number of the modern schools were organized by the great Śaṅkara in the first half of the ninth century. There are two main points to be noticed: (*a*) Modern practice is a combination of the practice of the hermit and the monk. The modern ascetic, or *sādhu*, as we shall call him, is supposed to be cut off from the world like the monk, but, like the hermit, he does not give up worship. (*b*) Most sādhus are sectarians: they are devotees of Vishṇu or of Śiva. There are several orders, notably the *Ekadaṇḍīs*, or One-rod Sannyāsīs, to which Śaṅkara belonged (see fig. 30), and the *Tridaṇḍīs*, or Three-rod Sannyāsīs, to which Rāmānuja belonged (see figs. 31 and 38), which are restricted to Brāhmans. These conform in most points to the ancient

42. MODERN TAPAS

This sādhu, being swung head downwards over a fire by a disciple, was photographed recently at Allahabad. (Photograph kindly favoured by Mr. E. M. Moffatt.)

rule of the monk; yet even they will be found worshipping one of the great gods. All the non-Brāhman orders reflect a number of other characteristics of modern Hinduism: they believe in pilgrimage, and often wear showy tokens of the great *tīrthas*, or places of pilgrimage, which they have

43. MODERN ŚIVAITE SĀDHU

His body is smeared with ashes. He was under a vow of silence and would not answer questions except with guttural grunts. He would not touch money, but a friend who happened to be near accepted a few coppers and promised to buy him some food. Photographed outside the temple of Rāmeśvara at Bhuvaneśvara. (Photograph kindly given by Mr. Frank Anderson, Bombay.)

visited. They carry symbols of their gods. A Vishṇuite will carry a *śālagrāma* stone, a discus, or an image of Rāma or Kṛishṇa. A Śivaite will smear his body with ashes like Śiva, and carry a trident, a tiger's skin, or a human skull. Many keep up the old forms of self-torture.

Asceticism has greatly deteriorated in modern times. There is no serious thought-movement in it; a large proportion of sādhus are ignorant men; many are grossly immoral; some of the orders are coarse and indecent; and Hindus acknowledge that there are but few sincere and earnest men amongst them. Yet here and there one meets a man of character and learning.

NOTE.—The text at the bottom of the page is the rule of THE ANCIENT WANDERING MONK, *parivrājaka*: 'He shall have neither fire nor dwelling; he may go to the village to get his food by begging; he shall be indifferent, not irresolute, a man of meditation and of concentration of mind.' *Mānava Dharmaśāstra*, vi. 43.

अनग्निरनिकेतः स्याद्ग्राममन्नार्थमाश्रयेत् ।
उपेक्षकोऽसंकसुको मुनिर्भावसमाहितः ॥

PART II

HINDUISM AS A SYSTEM

सर्वलक्षणहीनोऽपि यः सदाचारवान्नरः ।
श्रद्दधानोऽनसूयश्च शतं वर्षाणि जीवति ॥

CHAPTER XIV

WHAT IT IS TO BE A HINDU TO-DAY

A MAN is a Hindu because of two things, birth and conformity.

110. *Birth.* In order to be a Hindu, a man must have been born in one of the social groups which historically have become associated together in Hinduism, chiefly under Brāhman supervision, and which are known as castes. A European may call himself a Hindu, because he believes certain Hindu doctrines; but, according to all Hindu books and all Hindu usage, it is absolutely impossible for him to become a Hindu.

111. *Conformity.* In order to remain a Hindu, a man born in Hinduism must conform to the usages of the group in which he was born. The customs of the various castes vary to an extraordinary degree. In some castes a great many things are obligatory, in others comparatively few.

112. Conformity applies to four groups of actions :—

(*a*) MARRIAGE, FOOD, OCCUPATION, RESIDENCE. The rules about marriage are the most fundamental part of caste.

NOTE.—The text at the top of the page describes THE ORTHODOX HINDU : 'He who observes the usages established among the virtuous, who is a believer in revelation, and free from ill-will, lives a hundred years, even though he does not possess any external marks of prosperity.' *Vishṇusmṛiti*, lxxi. 92.

To marry outside one's caste is altogether forbidden; usually choice is further narrowed to one section or sub-caste; and even within this subdivision there are the further restrictions of *pravara* and *gotra*, which we need not explain here. To transgress any of the rules of marriage is the surest way to be excommunicated. Rules with regard to food restrict the articles of diet that may be eaten, the persons by whom food may be cooked, and the persons with whom it may be eaten. Educated men in the large cities usually keep caste rules about food in their own homes, but disregard them outside. Rules about occupation are in general very loose and easy among the educated classes, but very stringent where modern thought has not penetrated. An educated man may usually take up any occupation he pleases. The old law which forbade sea-voyages and residence outside India is being gradually laid aside by the higher castes.

(*b*) Domestic Ceremonies. The observance of certain domestic ceremonies is absolutely binding on every man who wishes to remain a Hindu. They are carried out with the utmost care in every family under the guidance of Brāhman priests.

In the code of Manu, as in the older sacred books, twelve domestic rites or sacraments, *saṁskāras*, are prescribed for the twice-born castes:—

(1) *Garbhādhāna*, impregnation, following the marriage ceremony.

(2) *Puṁsavana*, male-production, about three months after marriage.

(3) *Sīmantonnayana*, hair-parting, the parting of the woman's hair some time before the birth of her child.

(4) *Jāta-karman*, birth-ceremony.

(5) *Nāma-karaṇa*, name-giving.

(6) *Nishkramaṇa*, carrying-out. In the fourth month the child was carried out to look on the rising sun.

(7) *Anna-prāśana*, food-giving.

(8) *Chauḍa*, tonsure.

(9) *Keśānta*, hair-cutting.

(10) *Upanayana*, initiation, the ceremony which introduces the boy to his education. (See above, p. 42.)

(11) *Samāvartana*, home-coming, the return of the student to his home from the house of his teacher.

(12) *Vivāha*, marriage.

In the case of a girl there was no initiation, and the other ceremonies, with the exception of marriage, were performed without the recitation of sacred texts.

To-day the twice-born castes usually observe only the following:—

(5) *Nāma-karaṇa*, name-giving. } Usually observed to-
(7) *Anna-prāśana*, food-giving. } gether.

(10) *Upanayana*, initiation.

(12) *Vivāha*, marriage.

The other castes have corresponding ceremonies.

(*c*) ANCESTOR-WORSHIP. As we have seen in our first lesson, the Hindu family is patriarchal in form, because it rests on ancestor-worship. Modern customs differ a good deal in detail from the customs of the Ṛigvedic and earlier ages, yet in the main the ideas and the practice are the same.

Strictly speaking, the ceremonies connected with the burning of the dead do not, in the opinion of modern Hindus, come under the head of ancestor-worship. All primitive peoples believe that whoever touches a dead body is defiled thereby, and this idea still survives in all its strength in Hinduism. Hence the burning of the dead, which is called *antyeshṭi*, the last sacrifice, is polluting, and all the ceremonial connected with it is inauspicious; while the worship of ancestors is called *śrāddha*, an act of faith, and all the ceremonies that come under that head are auspicious. Yet the same fundamental belief and practice are visibly present in both.

The Funeral Ceremonies last ten days. The essential element in each day's ceremony is the offering of a *piṇḍa*, i. e. a ball of cooked rice, to the spirit of the deceased. The first is offered on the first day, before the body is burnt, and one is offered each of the other days. The belief is that the spirit of the deceased through feeding on this food acquires a gross body, *sthūla śarīra*, and is thereby transformed from a *preta* or wandering ghost into a *pitṛi*, a father, one of the company of glorified ancestors.

Śrāddha Ceremonies. A man's relatives, male and female, on both his father's and his mother's side, for three generations upward and three generations downward, are called his *sapiṇḍas*, i. e. 'sharers in the *piṇḍa*', because they take part in the *śrāddha* ceremonies with him. On the eleventh day, all the *sapiṇḍas* gather in the house of the person who is holding the ceremony, and an elaborate ceremony is conducted, the central element of which is the offering of a *piṇḍa* to every deceased person within the circle of *sapiṇḍas*. A feast follows the ceremony.

This is repeated monthly for one year, and then annually. These are obligatory. There are many other forms of *śrāddha* which may be undertaken if one choose.

(*d*) Worship of the Gods. Rules about worship vary very much amongst the lower castes of Hinduism, but among the upper castes they run on the following lines:—

(1) *Daily prayers, connected with bathing and teeth-cleaning, and daily sacrifices.* These are all observed by

strictly orthodox Hindus, but are often altogether neglected by educated men.

(2) *The daily worship of the household gods.* Usually the women see to this.

(3) *The recurrent festivals, fasts, and holy days.* These vary very greatly in different parts of the country and in the different sects. No Hindu can avoid taking part in these from time to time.

(4) *The worship of the temple.* This takes a large place in the lives of all Hindus except modern educated men, who very seldom go near a temple at all, at least in the North.

113. *Belief is altogether free.* A Hindu is generally understood to believe that the Vedas are inspired, that the Brāhmans are divinely appointed priests, and that caste is a divine institution, but a man may declare that he believes none of these things and yet remain a good Hindu, provided he conforms. Yet the stability of Hinduism depends in the last resort on the existence of these beliefs. Conformity, however, involves a practical acceptance of the Vedas, the Brāhmans, and caste; for the Vedas are quoted frequently in the domestic ceremonies, and the presence of Brāhmans is necessary for the right performance of each one of them.

114. Although Hinduism has many gods, many theologies, and many sacred books, a man may remain an orthodox Hindu without believing in any god or any theology, and without knowing or acknowledging a single sacred book. He must give some sort of practical recognition to some god or gods in the domestic ceremonies and family festivals, but the divinities thus reverenced vary all over India; there is no uniformity. Nor are there any theological conceptions which he need hold: an orthodox Hindu may be an atheist, an agnostic, or a Christian in his conception of the world. The sacred books of Hinduism are not read in the services of the temples, nor is the ordinary Hindu expected to

study them. They are for the priest and the philosopher. The *Rāmāyaṇa* and the *Mahābhārata*, however, are very largely read in the homes of the people.

115. But, although there is no set of beliefs which the Hindu as a Hindu is expected to hold, there are certain ideas or convictions which all or nearly all Hindus except those permeated by Western thought will be found to hold. There are perhaps three which may be classed together as being nearly as universal as Hinduism. They are, first, the validity of caste and the authority of the Vedas and the Brāhmans; second, the doctrine of transmigration; and third, the sacredness of the cow. Perhaps it may be said that a further general characteristic of Hinduism is to be found in a tendency of thought, feeling, and aspiration of which the logical issue is a mystic pantheism; but the degree in which pantheistic belief is explicit seems to vary very greatly.

Most Hindus are also touched at least in some degree with ascetic ideas. The villager, no matter how worldly his own life may be, is ready to affirm that the things of the world are worthless, that nothing is of any final value except God and the knowledge of God. He therefore holds that the man who does not give up the world in its entirety and become an ascetic does not really love God. He regards the preservation of animal life (*ahiṁsā*) as meritorious. (See section 23.)

116. Hindus are under the sway of innumerable superstitions. With the exception of the cultured few, the whole people live in terror of evil spirits. A great deal of the ordinary worship of the home and the temple is directed against their malign designs and influences; while at every step one meets the magic word and the magic spell, the charmed act and the charm hung round the neck, to prevent or repel the assault of the *bhūta*, the evil spirit. Amongst

the uneducated everywhere the Brāhman also is regarded with extreme superstitious fear: there is no limit to the powers of evil he is believed to control; so that the humble villager is kept in subjection and terror. Though the simplest Hindu is ready to express belief in one God only, his practical daily religion is a very vivid conviction that the idol in his village is alive, and not only eats, drinks, and sleeps but has power to bless or curse him in every detail of his life. The actual belief of to-day still is that the gods subsist on the sacrifices and offerings made to them, just as the spirits of dead ancestors are believed to live on the *piṇḍas* offered in the *śrāddha* and the *tarpaṇa*, water, offered in the daily ceremonies. The souls of the kids offered in sacrifice to the goddess *Kālī* are believed to go straight to heaven. Vishṇu is believed to be present in great power in every *śālagrāma* stone, a kind of black ammonite found in the Gaṇḍak river, and in every *tulsī* plant. Śiva and the other gods have similar superstitions attached to them. Indeed, there is no limit to the animals, trees, stones, rivers, wells in which divinities are believed to reside. The belief in holy times and places is quite as vigorous. Nor are these merely the picturesque fancies of Arcadian simplicity: they are powerful beliefs, sanctioned in very large measure by the highest Hindu authorities, taught in the literature and by the priests, and governing men's lives.

NOTE.—The text at the bottom of the page summarizes THE RELIGIOUS DUTY OF THE HINDU: 'Let him worship according to the rule, the sages by the private recitation of the Veda, the gods by burnt oblations, the fathers by funeral offerings, men by gifts of food, and the spirits by the *bali* offering.' *Mānava Dharmaśāstra*, iii. 81.

स्वाध्यायेनार्चयेतर्षीन् होमैर्देवान्यथाविधि ।
पितॄञ्छ्राद्धेन नॄनन्नैर्भूतानि बलिकर्मणा ॥

चण्डालश्वपचानां तु बहिर्ग्रामात्प्रतिश्रयः ।
अवपात्राश्च कर्तव्या धनमेषां श्वगर्दभम् ॥

CHAPTER XV

THE RELIGION OF THE LOWER CLASSES

117. The lower orders of the population of India fall into two great classes, those who have lived in close contact with Hindu society, and those who have lived apart in the mountains and forests. The latter have retained their old religion and social organization, but the former have all succumbed to the influence of caste and have absorbed large elements of Hindu theology, mythology, and superstition.

118. Those peoples who have lived an isolated life and have in consequence not come under Hindu influence need be only mentioned here, as they do not naturally come into a study of Hinduism. We may just mention the names of the chief tribes. They are—the Santāls, the Orāons, the Juangs, and the Kols of Western Bengal; the Garos, Khāsis, and Nāgas of Assam; the Khonds of Orissa; the Gonds and Bhils of Central India; and the Todas and other hill tribes in the Madras Presidency.

119. The other class of tribes, however, have been decidedly Hinduized both socially and religiously, and there-

NOTE.—The text at the top of the page refers to THE UNCLEAN CASTES: 'But the dwelling of Chaṇḍālas and Śvapachas shall be outside the village; vessels used by them must be thrown away; and their wealth shall be dogs and donkeys.' *Mānava Dharmaśāstra*, x. 51.

fore they must receive our attention. Being organized in castes, they necessarily vary to a considerable extent in social standing. Certain castes are allowed to visit Brāhmanical temples, and thus belong to the central mass of Hindus. These acknowledge the great Hindu gods and

44. SHRINE OF CHENGALAMMA

Chengalamma is a village goddess propitiated in times of trouble. She is somehow identified with the Margosa tree, and the square pattern made with red and yellow powder represents her. The ant-hill is the home of a cobra worshipped by the villagers as a Nāga. (Photographed for the author.)

conform to Hindu usage as far as they possibly can. Yet even these recognized castes worship many divinities which no Brāhman would have anything to do with.

120. There are, on the other hand, vast multitudes of people in both north and south who are regarded as unclean

who are in consequence excluded from all Brāhmanical temples, and for whom no Brāhman will perform any ceremony (see section 45). High-caste Hindus usually refuse the title Hindu altogether to these races; but they have come so largely under Hindu influence that they cannot be excluded from a study of the religion. They show this

45. SHRINE OF BONTALA GANGAMMA

A wayside goddess at whose shrine a weary traveller deposits a rag and a stone, in order that he may lose his fatigue. (Photographed for the author.)

Hindu influence first of all in their caste organization and in their social usages, which are very largely an imitation of high-caste practice; secondly, in their belief in Hindu theology and superstition, and their desire to bring their village divinities into some sort of relation to the great gods of the Hindu pantheon.

The lowest of these castes are held in such abhorrence that they are not allowed to live beside the higher castes. They form villages for themselves.

121. Both of these Hinduized groups are inclined to pay worship to the lower divinities of Hinduism, Gaṇeśa and Skanda (also called Kārttikeya and Subrahmaṇya), the sons of Śiva, who are believed to be of great service against

46. SHRINE AND STAKE OF POTU-RĀJU

This deity is usually spoken of as the brother or husband of the village goddess. He is propitiated when danger threatens. The small stone represents the gods. The pointed pillar is really a stake on which the villagers used to impale the animals offered to him as propitiation. (Photograph kindly given by the Rev. W. T. Elmore.)

demons, and above all Kālī, the black, bloodthirsty, goddess of the North, who is identified with the wife of Śiva. Hanumān, the monkey-god, who is connected with agriculture, is very widely reverenced; and other divine animals, especially Nandi, Śiva's bull, and the divine serpents called Nāgas: see fig. 5, p. 60, fig. 10, p. 81, and fig. 44, p. 185. Trees are worshipped all over India, and certain sacred stones.

122. But the worship to which the ignorant Indian villager clings with most fervour is just the village divinity. These are found all over India, varying everywhere, yet retaining certain broad similarities everywhere. The points that are most worthy of notice with regard to these much honoured gods are as follows :—

(*a*) Each is a local divinity, attached to the village, and reverenced for that reason. The gods of Hinduism, on the other hand, have usually a much wider vogue.

47. SHRINE OF POTU-RĀJU
(Photographed for the author.)

(*b*) The priests of these divinities are not Brāhmans, but men of all castes.

(*c*) The great majority of these divinities are goddesses. In the South almost every one has the word *amma*, 'mother,' in her name. They are thus known as the Mothers.

(*d*) They are propitiated rather than adored. Visitations of disease, famine, earthquake, &c., are attributed to them ; and special sacrifices and festivals are held to induce them to remove the scourge. Animals are usually sacrificed to them on these occasions, fowls, sheep, goats, pigs, and buffaloes.

(*e*) In the South each goddess has usually one, if not more, male attendants, but they are subordinate to her.

(*f*) In the Tamil country in South India a god named Iyenar is found in most villages. He is the village watch-

48. SHRINE OF POLERAMMA

Poleramma is the protectress of the village boundary. (Photograph kindly given by the Rev. W. T. Elmore.)

man. He is supposed to ride round the village by night, driving away demons. Animals are never sacrificed to him. Images of horses are set up at his shrine as dedicatory offerings.

(*g*) The shrines of these divinities are of the rudest description, often only a small piece of land marked off by lines of stones. Frequently there is no symbol of the god at all; often a stained stone is set up; often a rude image.

The illustrations in the text are all from the Telugu country.

123. The people suffer greatly from their fear of evil spirits; insomuch that a very large part of their religion consists in efforts to drive them away or to nullify their influence.

49. THE UNCLEANNESS OF THE OUTCASTE

This outcaste woman has come to make a purchase, but she dare not approach the merchant, far less enter the shop. From a distance she tells what she wants, lays down the money and then goes away still farther. The merchant brings out the goods, takes the money and retires. The woman then comes and takes away her purchase. (The author owes this photograph to the kindness of Mr. Henri Schaetti.)

GOD THAT MADE THE WORLD HATH MADE OF ONE BLOOD ALL NATIONS OF MEN

येनास्य पितरो याता येन याताः पितामहाः।
तेन यायात्सतां मार्गं तेन गच्छन्न रिष्यते ॥

CHAPTER XVI

FORMATIVE ELEMENTS OF HINDUISM

124. If we are to understand the spirit of Hinduism, it is necessary first of all to learn to sympathize with the immeasurable reverence which the Hindu feels for the social organization of his people. He believes that the constitution of the family and the organization of society go back to time immemorial; and modern research has in a measure justified the claim. Ancestor-worship and the patriarchal family date from the days when the Aryan people were still undivided; and, while caste is a more recent growth, the spirit and principles of caste lie at the basis of all early society. To the Hindu, therefore, these things are sacred in the extreme, priceless in value, so much a part of the life of the people that they must on no account be disturbed. The old-world reverence for what is customary and settled, which was once universal, has been preserved in Hindu life unchanged down to our own days.

Then, again, to the Hindu, as to the ancient Aryan, and to all early peoples, what we call moral laws are rather sacred customs which have been traditionally observed from

NOTE.—The text at the top of the page gives THE LAW OF CUSTOM: 'Let him walk in that path of holy men which his father and his grandfathers followed; while he walks in that, he will not suffer harm.' *Mānava Dharmaśāstra*, iv. 178.

time immemorial than eternal principles of the moral life. These customs are inextricably interwoven with the special forms of family life and social organization which have created the people. To tamper with them is therefore to be guilty at once of sacrilege and of treason against the life of the race.

But these customs, though regarded as inviolably sacred and absolutely essential for the well-being of the people which practises them, are not regarded as binding on other peoples: other customs may be necessary for them, and therefore sacred and inviolable to them. The early peoples did not possess the conception of a lofty moral law by which all customs and all men are judged; nor did they think of their own moral customs as being in any sense binding on the gods. They were above morality.

We ought also to notice that there is a very large and very serious historical reason for this permanent attitude of the Hindu to the foundations of Hindu society. The race has been preserved amid the countless military and political changes of India by its faithful adherence to the traditional family and caste life. Of that there can be no question. The Chinese people have had a similar experience, and they are filled with a similar reverence. Thus, the old attitude is very largely justifiable; but the changed circumstances of India render a new attitude most necessary to-day, as all thoughtful leaders see.

On the other hand, it is this lofty belief in the sacredness of custom that has shielded all the abuses of family-life and caste-life in India. When a custom is believed to have come down from early times, the obligation to observe it seems to the ordinary Hindu to be absolutely beyond dispute. To break away from it in his eyes is tantamount to a revolt against society. Hence child-marriage, compulsory widowhood, widow-burning, widow-drudgery, female infanticide and the thousand inhuman cruelties of caste were in the past regarded as inviolably sacred, even by the thinking Hindu.

125. The main idea which the Hindu has with regard to worship is that every god must be worshipped according to his own wishes. The command of a god must be honoured, no matter what it may be. The Hindu mind possessed no settled conception as to the moral or religious character of the gods; and consequently no man could tell beforehand what might be demanded by any god or goddess in the way of worship.

The origin of the great gods of the Aryan peoples will make this idea still clearer. They were originally powers of nature, and therefore had *natural* attributes. Sun and wind, fire and rain had no necessary connexion with morality. But they were powers, and therefore to be honoured and pacified by men. One could not guess beforehand what their wishes might be; but it was man's interest to gratify them, whatever form of worship they desired, whatever kind of action they ordained.

The conception of *Brahman* which inspires the Upanishads also illustrates the point. In chapter v we found that *Brahman* is thought of as reality, intelligence, and joy, but not as righteousness. Yet the Upanishads are the very summit of Hindu thought. Thus moral character was in no sense a part of the Vedic conception of God.

This explains the fact that new forms of worship were constantly admitted into Hinduism, once the people began to spread over India. So long as the practice of the new cult did not come into violent collision with the ancient organization of the family and society and with the old customs connected therewith, there was no objection raised. It was quite probable that one of the innumerable gods had appeared and had given instructions for the institution of the new cult.

We are now in a position to realize how it has been possible for the Hindu to admit such things as the following into his worship:—unlimited idolatry, human sacrifice, cruel torture, temple prostitution, and obscene sculpture. The same idea explains how the Hindu did not regard it as unbecoming that Kālī should be the patron divinity of robbers and murderers. From the same point of view we can realize how the gross and grotesque images of the gods were possible. There was no definite conception in the Hindu mind as to what a god must be; and consequently any form might conceivably represent some divine power. All this lack of a limiting moral conception will also enable us to understand how the coarse myths of the *Mahābhārata* and the *Purāṇas* were attributed to the gods, and how the ancient ascetics could believe that the tortures they endured were of real value.

126. As among all early peoples, so among Hindus orthodoxy is *conformity to religious custom* and not any form of belief. The man who does what is demanded of him to the gods, to his ancestors, to his family, and to society is a good Hindu, no matter what he believes. This is quite comprehensible: it is only when spiritual religion arises that men realize the religious importance of the state of a man's mind. Character too stands in no definite relation to Hindu orthodoxy. A man may be guilty of gross immoralities and yet may be in good standing in his caste and his family; while a man of the noblest character who breaks a caste-law, however absurd or inhuman it may be, will be outcasted. In Mysore, where Christian baptism still deprives a man of his property, there were two brothers. One was a man of high character, but he had become a Christian; the other was an orthodox Hindu, but was lying in prison undergoing a sentence for some crime. The Christian was disinherited, and the criminal got his property. This is in strict accordance with Hindu principle. The law-books contain many pieces of moral advice, but they scarcely touch the organization of the family or society.

127. Thus far we have dealt with the principles lying at the basis of the ancient faith in its unmixed state as it still survives among the ignorant classes all over the country. But, as we have seen, the growth of culture and the conquest of India produced at a very early date a cataclysmal revolution in Hindu thought. A great new theology was built up which set forth the one Reality over against the mirage of the world, and put forward transmigration and Karma as the explanation of the sorrows and inequalities of human life. From this upheaval came the whole philosophic movement within Hinduism, with its speculative theories, on the one hand, and its ascetic renunciation, on the other. Wherever the Brāhman has gone, he has carried with him some slight sketch of this new theology; and in consequence it has become diffused generally throughout India. Ascetics have proved a powerful object-lesson to the common people. Hence, there are a number of great religious ideas which are held by most Hindus and which have had a certain influence over the mind of the people. Perhaps, the most prominent of these principles are:—(1) the vanity of the world, (2) the supremacy of the spiritual life, and (3) the nobility of asceticism. Men have believed that only the man who is willing to give up everything for God is a true saint. Union with God has been the spiritual ideal of the people.

The various theistic movements have greatly enriched the religious life of India. The belief in a personal God, in His love and grace and in the possibility of personal intercourse with Him has helped multitudes of Hindus to live a life of real religious joy and peace. *Bhakti* has been a source of deep spiritual feeling, first to many educated men, and then to the thousands of the common people who have followed Rāmānanda, Kabīr, Tulsī Dās, and the rest.

128. Yet, strange to say, these spiritual movements, pantheistic and theistic, have failed utterly to spiritualize the Hindu faith. Popular Hinduism remains to this day gross, materialistic, idolatrous, and often obscene. How are we to account for the fact that the new thought has touched deeply only the minority and has failed to transform the life, the thought, and the religion of the masses? There are several reasons for this gigantic failure:—

(*a*) The very pantheism which satisfies the Vedāntist justifies polytheism and idolatry. If you do not know Brahman, you must stick to your idols. So Indian theism, even the theism of Rāmānuja and Tulsī Dās, has never been seriously monotheistic. The god chosen for the place of the Supreme is set above all others, but the rest retain their divine position and form a happy family around him. The only Hindu reformer who is a serious monotheist is Kabīr, and he is half a Muḥammadan. Even Nānak, the founder of Sikhism, acknowledges the whole Hindu pantheon.

(*b*) The doctrine of transmigration has been a serious hindrance in two distinct ways. First, it suggests that a man's moral and spiritual state is scarcely under his own control, since it is the result of his past life: so that it is quite possible that he is not yet in a fit state for accepting a spiritual religion. Secondly, it suggests that, since a man will have many more lives, there will be plenty of opportunity for repentance in the future.

(*c*) The ascetic cut himself adrift from human society, on the ground that ordinary human life is altogether secular and unspiritual. The religion of the race thus fell into two halves, the religion of the people and the religion of the monk; and as the religion of the people was considered utterly useless to the spiritual man, those who had risen to the higher life did not dream of exerting themselves to better that which seemed to them hopeless.

(*d*) Since there was no moral element in the Vedic conception of God, the worship of God produced no compelling conviction in the mind of the worshipper that he was in duty bound to serve his fellow men. The ascetic is not a servant of humanity.

129. Hindu morality grew with the culture of the race, and many a tributary rill of thought passed from philosophy, asceticism, and the higher theology, into the common mind of the people. Above all, Buddhism left a large moral legacy to Hinduism. There is much that is beautiful in family life, despite its many blots. The Hindu is charitable, peaceful, law-abiding. He honours religion and believes no nation can be built without it. Thus Hindu morality, as found in the best books and in the life of orthodox families, has many high qualities. The modern Hindu who has drunk of Western thought in Indian or European universities also maintains that Hindu morality has a solid spiritual basis in Hindu philosophy; that from that starting-point man's moral relation to God and his complete responsibility to God may be clearly worked out. This is strange, if it be true; for it is certain no one attempted to find such things in Hindu philosophy until Christian thought appeared in India.

NOTE.—The text at the bottom of the page gives the sum of the Vedānta:—

> The hard-to-see, the mystery-hidden,
> Heart-dwelling, cave-abiding, old—
> He who by brooding o'er his inner self
> Sees Him as God escapes both joy and grief.
>
> *Kāṭhaka Upanishad*, ii. 12.

तं दुर्दर्शं गूढमनुप्रविष्टं गुहाहितं गह्वरेष्ठं पुराणम्।
अध्यात्मयोगाधिगमेन देवं मत्वा धीरो हर्षशोकौ जहाति॥

CHAPTER XVII

THE FUTURE OF HINDUISM

130. Note the extraordinary strength of Hinduism :—

(*a*) Like Chinese ancestor-worship, it has held the people firmly together for millenniums, while other civilized races of the ancient world have gone to pieces.

(*b*) It has had to meet hostile attacks of overwhelming strength, and yet it has in each case won the victory: note especially Buddhism, Jainism, Muḥammadanism.

Its strength lies mainly in three elements :—

(*a*) *Its family system*, founded on ancestor-worship. This links each generation with the past and the future, and binds living members closely together. To give this up seems disloyalty to one's ancestors and gross impiety towards other members of the family.

(*b*) *Its caste system.* This is strong in several ways. It is founded on original race and culture divergencies as distinct as those that now sever European and Hindu: a man

NOTE.—The head-piece above is a scroll from Gandhāran sculpture. Foucher, *L'Art Gréco-Bouddhique du Gandhāra*, fig. 103. (See above, section 53.)

thus feels that he has an aristocratic stronghold in his caste, and also a certainty of the purity of his birth and of his customs. Caste has preserved the forms of ancient society almost unchanged into our day: it has thus the strength of immemorial custom. A Hindu feels that to go out of caste is practically to go out of civilization. The outcaste often finds life almost impossible.

(*c*) *Its religious system*, which must be acknowledged to be the highest form which polytheism has ever taken. It teaches a lofty conception of the world; it brings every detail of life under the rule of religion; and it has certain very beautiful ideas in connexion with home life, notwithstanding its degradation of women. Its strength lies largely in the fact that it justifies every form of traditional worship, and yet offers forms of spiritual faith to those who want such. It thus gathers to itself all the strength of custom and habit, and disturbs no one with serious demands. It can attract almost every type of mind; for it offers a response to almost every form of religious need.

131. If modern thought and Western influence could be kept out of India, Hinduism might go on indefinitely, only changing slowly as it has changed in the past. But modern thought, as introduced by missions, education, and Western influence generally, has begun to weaken Hinduism as no force active in India in earlier centuries ever did:—

(*a*) The office clerk performs the *śrāddha* for his father, but he no longer believes in its efficacy. Thus faith in the religious basis of the Hindu family has faded out of the minds of educated Hindus.

(*b*) Our modern knowledge of the different races of the world and of the way in which they rise and fall in the scale of civilization has made it impossible for any thinking man to believe the ancient Hindu doctrine, that the four castes are divinely appointed and permanent institutions, and that it is a religious duty to observe the rules of caste. Educated Hindus frequently seek to defend caste as healthy in certain ways, but they do not pretend to believe the old doctrine. They never declare that it is wrong for a man who is not a Brāhman to teach religion.

The national movement with its demand for equality and its summons to union is everywhere weakening caste.

(*c*) Educated men defend idolatry as being a help to the ignorant, but they never say that they actually believe in the existence of the *devas* represented by the idols. Polytheism has become incredible.

Compare the conditions which obtained in the Roman Empire, while Christianity was in its death-struggle with the old religions.

132. Thus if the modern spirit is to remain in India, and education is to be extended, it is only a question of how long time the process of collapse will take. The religious foundations of Hinduism (namely, the rules of caste, the authority of the Veda, the authority of Brāhmans, polytheism, and idolatry) crumble to pieces in the atmosphere of modern thought. They are, one and all, old-world superstitions, which fade away in the light of modern truth.

We may therefore be perfectly certain that, unless some unforeseen revolution occurs to seclude India more securely than before from modern influences, belief in the essentials of Hinduism is bound to decay as surely as belief in witches and other fears have disappeared at home.

But, though honest belief in these basal doctrines is certain to gradually disappear, most men will for a long time continue to remain within Hinduism: and all sorts of new defences will be hastily flung up around the old camp to save it from being stormed. The first great attempt in this direction is being made now by Mrs. Besant and the Bhārat Dharma Mahāmandal.

As decay increases, however, the number of honest men who feel they cannot remain in a hypocritical position will steadily increase; and the interest of the problem lies in them: where will they turn? Which religion will they adopt?

133. The position of affairs is most interesting. We have seen in chapters iii and iv how the early Indo-Aryans, as their ancient tribal experience became widened by the conquest of India and their intercourse with many races and many religions, were compelled to transform their fundamental conceptions, and to produce a new theology, which we dealt with in chapter iv under the name of Essential Hinduism. Similarly in these modern days, the widened experience, the new knowledge, and the fresh moral ideas begotten from contact with European religion, education, and government, and from the impact of the world's commerce on the economic life of India, are making another and more radical reconstruction of Indian ideas altogether inevitable. The old pantheistic thought does not thrive well in the new ethical atmosphere; the idea of progress makes the old Hindu conception of cyclic change appear childish and old-fashioned; transmigration does not seem such a solid and certain doctrine as it once seemed; and modern thought simply destroys faith in the many gods of paganism and the value of idols. Thinking Indians must inevitably form new conceptions of God, man, morality, religion, and the meaning of the world.

134. Hence, we may be perfectly certain that ancient Hindu thought cannot survive. Something else will take its place. A new religion must be found, a religion which will—

(*a*) Provide a religious foundation for the wider and truer ideas which now dominate the Hindu mind;

(*b*) Satisfy the religious instincts of the people, and stimulate them to purity, progress, and strength.

Christianity is unquestionably the source of the new explosive thought which is recreating the Indian character and intellect to-day. There is no other religion that contains these master ideas. Only in the riches of Christianity —Christ and His cross, the Fatherhood of God, the Brotherhood of man, and the Kingdom of God—can Hindus find the universal principles needed for a new intellectual, moral, and social life.

Except Christianity, there is no religion in the whole world that is rich enough in theology, worship, emotion, literature to take the place of Hinduism.

135. We need not attempt to prophesy the day nor the hour when these vast changes will work themselves out. There may be no sudden outburst for a long time, but rather a continuous increase in the momentum of the movement towards Christianity. The progress of the faith in other lands will have an influence on India which it is at present impossible to estimate. We may expect great developments within Hinduism, a stubborn and prolonged resistance from the central party, but an abundant victory for Christ in the end.

NOTE.—The tail-piece below is a scroll of bo-tree leaves from Gandhāra. Foucher, fig. 95. (See above, section 53.)

BIBLIOGRAPHY

The following brief list of books is meant to guide the student in the early stages of his work. For this reason a good many references are given to sections and chapters of books, in order to make effective study possible with a few volumes. Many books which are out of print are mentioned, as they may be found in libraries or purchased second-hand. For information as to original texts, readers are referred to the Bibliography at the end of Macdonell's *Sanskrit Literature*. In the case of books published in India, Indian prices are always given. Where English prices are given also, they are the prices at which the books may be got from booksellers in Britain. The following abbreviations are used:—

Encyclopædia of Religion and Ethics.	*E.R.E.*
Grundriss der Indo-Arischen Philologie und Altertumskunde, or *Encyclopædia of Indo-Aryan Research.* Published in parts, some of which are in English, some in German. Strasburg: Trübner.	*Grundriss*
Sacred Books of the East.	*S.B.E.*
Journal of the Royal Asiatic Society.	*J.R.A.S.*

I. General Works.

(*a*) Hinduism.

1. *Hinduism.* By L. D. Barnett, M.A., D.Litt. Constable & Co. 1*s.* Every student ought to have this sketch.

2. *The Religions of India.* By E. W. Hopkins, Ph.D. Ginn & Co. 8*s.* 6*d.* net.

The most recent manual of Hinduism. Contains much valuable material rather loosely arranged.

3. *The Religions of India.* By A. Barth. Translated by the Rev. J. Wood. Trübner. 16*s.*

Older than Hopkins's book, but written with all the clearness of the best French work.

4. *The Religious Sects of the Hindus.* Compiled by the late Dr. John Murdoch largely from Prof. H. H. Wilson's famous sketch. Christian Literature Society. (As. 6.) 9*d.*

A mine of information. Criticism occasionally harsh.

(*b*) Hindu Literature.

5. *The Imperial Gazetteer of India.* Vol. ii. Clarendon Press. 6*s*. net.

A volume containing chapters by different writers on Epigraphy, Archaeology, Coinage, Literature, Architecture, and History. Chap. VI is an outline of the history of Sanskrit literature, while Chap. XI is a very useful sketch of vernacular literature.

6. *A History of Sanskrit Literature.* By A. A. Macdonell, M.A., Ph.D. Heinemann. 6*s*.

The best manual on the literature.

7. *A Literary History of India.* By R. W. Frazer, LL.B. Fisher Unwin. 12*s*. 6*d*. net.

An attractive volume, weaving the chief books, both Sanskrit and vernacular, into the history of India.

8. *A History of Ancient Sanskrit Literature.* By Max Müller. Reprinted, Allahabad, Pāṇini Office, 1912. Rs. 6.

In spite of its age this great work is still most useful for reference on Vedic literature.

9. *The Heart of India.* By L. D. Barnett, M.A., Litt.D. John Murray. 2*s*.

A series of useful extracts from Hindu literature, both Sanskrit and vernacular.

II. Prehistoric Times.

For the Aryan period see article, *Aryan Religion*, by Dr. Otto Schrader, *E.R.E.*, and for the Indo-Iranian period see Chap. III of No. 15.

III. The Vedas. (1) Introduction.

No. 6 contains sufficient introduction to each of the Vedas for the beginner.

10. *The Rigveda.* By Adolf Kaegi. Translated by R. Arrowsmith, Ph.D. 91 pages of text with 107 pages of closely printed notes. Boston: Ginn & Co. 6*s*. 6*d*.

11. *The Atharvaveda.* By Maurice Bloomfield. 136 pp. *Grundriss.* 7*s*.

(2) Translations.

12. *Rigveda, Sāmaveda, White Yajurveda, Atharvaveda.* Translated by R. T. H. Griffith, M.A., C.I.E. Benares: Lazarus. *Rigveda*, Rs. 14; *Sāmaveda*, Rs. 4; *White Yajur*, Rs. 3 as. 13; *Atharvan*, Rs. 12.

13. *Atharva-Veda-Samhitā.* Translated by W. D. Whitney and C. R. Lanman. 2 vols. Harvard Oriental Series. Ginn & Co. 21*s*. net.

(3) Life and Religion.

14. *Altindisches Leben.* By H. Zimmer. Berlin. 10 m.

15. *The Religion of the Veda.* By Maurice Bloomfield, Ph.D., LL.D. New York: Putnam's Sons. 6*s.*

IV. The Brāhmaṇas. (1) Introduction.

See pp. 202–18 of No. 6, and pp. 342–455 of No. 8. Part IV of No. 11 contains a helpful introduction to the *Gopatha Brāhmaṇa.* For the religion of these books see Chap. IX of No. 2, and for the sacrifices see Chap. V of No. 7.

(2) Translations.

16. *The Śatapatha Brāhmaṇa.* Translated by Julius Eggeling. Vols. xii, xxvi, xli, xliii, xliv of *S.B.E.* Each 12*s.* 6*d.* net. Vol. xliv, 18*s.* 6*d.* net.

V. Philosophic Period.

For general conditions read Chaps. I to VI of No. 93 below. For a sketch of the schools of the times see Chap. I of No. 96 below. A vivid picture of the Brāhmans is given in Chap. VIII of No. 7. For Buddhism and Jainism see below, sections xvii and xviii.

VI. The Āraṇyakas and Upanishads.

(1) Introduction.

17. *Brahma Knowledge.* By L. D. Barnett, M.A., Litt.D. John Murray. 2*s.*

An exposition of the teaching of the Upanishads, with a number of extracts from them.

18. *The Philosophy of the Upanishads.* By Paul Deussen. Translated by the Rev. A. S. Geden, M.A. T. & T. Clark. 10*s.* 6*d.*

The standard work.

(2) Translations.

19. *The Īśā, Kena, Kāṭhaka, Praśna, Muṇḍaka, and Māṇḍūkya Upanishads.* Text and translation. By S. C. Vasu. Allahabad: Pāṇini Office. Rs. 5.

20. *Upanishads* (the eleven classical treatises). Translated by Max Müller. *S.B.E.*, vols. i and xv. Each 10*s.* 6*d.* net.

21. *Sechzig Upanishad's des Veda.* Von Dr. Paul Deussen. Leipzig: Brockhaus. 20*s.*

A most reliable translation. Introductions very valuable also.

22. *Aitareya Āraṇyaka* (including the Upanishad). Introduction, text, translation, commentary. By A. B. Keith. Clarendon Press. 25*s.* net.

23. *Śāṅkhāyana Āraṇyaka.* Translated by A. B. Keith. Royal Asiatic Society. 5*s.*

(3) Concordance.

24. *Concordance to the Principal Upanishads and Bhagavadgītā.* By G. A. Jacob. Bombay: Government Book Dépôt. Rs. 8.

VII. The Sūtras. (1) Introduction.

25. *Ritual-Literatur, Vedische Opfer und Zauber.* Von A. Hillebrandt. *Grundriss.* 12s.

Chap. IX of No. 6 supplies a good historical introduction, and Chap. I of No. 8 still fuller information. Chap. XI of No. 2 gives a very helpful account of the popular religion reflected in these treatises.

(2) Translations.

26. *Gṛihya Sūtras* (eight treatises). Translated by Oldenberg and Müller. *S.B.E.*, vols. xxix and xxx. Each 12s. 6d. net.

27. *The Sacred Laws of the Āryas* (the Dharma-sūtras of Āpastamba, Gautama, Vasishṭha, and Baudhāyana). Translated by Georg Bühler *S.B.E.*, vols. ii. and xiv. Each 10s. 6d. net.

VIII. The Epics.

(a) *The Mahābhārata.* (1) Introduction.

28. *Das Mahābhārata.* Von A. Holtzmann. 4 vols. Kiel. 42 m.

29. *The Great Epic of India.* By E. W. Hopkins. Scribner's. $4 net.

Pages 277–98 of No. 6 provide sufficient introduction for the beginner, and thereafter 30 or 31 may be read.

(2) English Translations.

30. *The Mahābhārata and the Rāmāyaṇa*, condensed into English verse by R. C. Dutt. Dent, *Every Man's Library*, 1s.

31. *The Mahābhārata, an English Abridgment.* By John Murdoch, LL.D. Christian Literature Society. (As. 7.) 10d.

A useful outline of the vast poem. The criticism is crude.

32. *The Mahābhārata translated into English prose.* By Pratāp Chandra Ray. 11 volumes. Calcutta. Out of print.

(3) Vernacular Versions.

CENTURY	LANGUAGE	AUTHOR	TITLE
XII–XV	Telugu	Three writers	*Mahābhārata*
XV	Bengali	Kāśi Rām Dās	
XVI	Oṛiyā	Sāraḷā Dās	*Bhārata*
	Assamese	Rāma Sarasvatī	
XVII	Malayāḷam	Tuñjattu Eṛuttachchhan	
XVII	Gujarātī	Rewa-Śaṅkar	
XIX	Hindī	Gokulnāth	

(*b*) *The Rāmāyaṇa.* (1) Introduction.

33. *Das Rāmāyaṇa.* Von Hermann Jacobi. Bonn: Friedrich Cohen. 15 m.

Sufficient introduction for the beginner will be found in pages 302–17 of No. 6, and thereafter the student may read No. 30 or No. 34, or may take up the whole poem in No. 35.

(2) English Translations.

34. *The Rāmāyaṇa, an English Abridgment.* By John Murdoch, LL.D. Christian Literature Society. (As. 7.) 10*d.*

A handy sketch of the Epic. Criticism rather crude.

35. *The Rāmāyaṇa of Vālmīki, translated into English verse.* By Ralph T. H. Griffith, M.A., C.I.E. Benares: Lazarus. Rs. 6.

36. *The Rāmāyaṇa.* Translated into English prose by M. N. Dutt. 7 vols. Calcutta. £1 8*s.*

(3) Vernacular Versions.

CENTURY	LANGUAGE	AUTHOR	TITLE
XI	Tamil	Kamban	*Rāmāyaṇa*
	Kanarese	Kumāra Vālmīki	*Rāmāyaṇa*
XIV	Malayāḷam	—	*Rāma Charita*
XVI	Oṛiyā	Balarāma	*Rāmāyaṇa*
XVI	Bengali	Kīrtibas Ojhā	*Rāmāyaṇa*
XVI	Western Hindī	Keśav Dās	*Rāma Chandrikā*
	Assamese	Rāma Sarasvatī	*Rāmāyaṇa*
XVII	Hindī	Tulsī Dās	*Rāma Charit Manas*
XIX	Mārwāṛī	Manśā Rām	*Raghunāth Rūpak*

37. *Rāmāyaṇa of Tulsī Das, translated from the Original Hindi.* By F. S. Growse, M.A., C.I.E. 2 vols. Allahabad: Government Press. Rs. 8 as. 8.

IX. The Dharmaśāstras. (1) Introduction.

38. *Recht und Sitte.* Von J. Jolly. *Grundriss.* 9*s.*

Sufficient introduction for the beginner will be found in the Introduction to vol. xxv of *S.B.E.*, No. 39, and in pp. 263–9 and 348–433 of No. 2.

(2) Translations.

32. *Manu, Vishṇu, Nārada, Bṛihaspati.* Translated by Bühler and Jolly. *S.B.E.*, vols. vii, xxv, xxxiii. Vol. xxv out of print; the others 10*s.* 6*d.* each net.

X. The Philosophies.

(*a*) General Introduction.

40. *The Six Systems of Indian Philosophy.* By Max Müller. Longmans. 7*s.* 6*d.* net.

Beginners will find sufficient information in Chap. XV of No. 6, and in the Introduction to No. 57.

41. *Sarva Darśana Saṅgraha.* By Mādhava. Translated by Cowell and Gough. Trübner. 10*s.* 6*d.*

(*b*) Karma Mīmāṁsā.

42. *The Mīmāṁsā Sūtras of Jaimini.* Translated into English by Gaṅga Nāth Jhā. Allahabad: Pāṇini Office. Being published in parts.

(*c*) Vedānta. (1) The System.

43. *Outline of the Vedānta System of Philosophy.* By Dr. Paul Deussen. Luzac. 4*s.* 6*d.*

44. *Das System des Vedānta.* Von Dr. Paul Deussen. Leipzig: Brockhaus. 12 m.

(2) Translations.

45. *The Vedānta-sūtras with Śaṅkara's Commentary.* Translated by George Thibaut. *S.B.E.*, vols. xxxiv and xxxviii. 12*s.* 6*d.* each.

46. *The Vedānta-sūtras with Rāmānuja's Commentary.* Translated by George Thibaut. *S.B.E.*, vol. xlviii. 25*s.*

47. *The Vedānta-sūtras with the Śaiva Bhāshya of Nīlakaṇṭha.* Being published. Madras: Meykaṇḍan Press.

48. *The Vedānta-sūtras with the Commentary of Madhva.* Translated by S. Subha Rao. Madras: Natesan. Rs. 3 as. 8.

49. *The Vedānta-sūtras with Baladeva's Commentary.* Translated by S. C. Vasu. Allahabad: Pāṇini Office. Rs. 10 as. 8.

50. *A Manual of Hindu Pantheism, the Vedāntasāra.* Translated with notes by G. A. Jacob. Trübner. 6*s.*

(*d*) Sāṅkhya and Yoga. (1) The System.

51. *Sāṅkhya und Yoga.* Von R. Garbe. *Grundriss.* 3*s.* 6*d.*

(2) Translations.

52. *Hindu Philosophy, the Sāṅkhya Kārikā.* Translated by John Davies. Trübner. 6*s.*

53. *The Sāṅkhya Aphorisms of Kapila.* Translated by J. R. Ballantyne. Trübner. 16*s.*

54. *Patañjali's Yoga Sūtras,* with Commentaries. Translated by Rāma Prashād. Allahabad: Pāṇini Office. Rs. 4 as. 8.

(*e*) Vaiśeshika.

55. *The Vaiśeshika-sūtras of Kaṇāda with Commentaries.* Translated by Nanda Lal Sinha. Allahabad: Pāṇini Office. Rs. 7.

(*f*) **Nyāya.**

56. *The Nyāya Sūtras of Gotama in English.* Allahabad: Pāṇini Office. Rs. 1 as. 8.

XI. THE BHAGAVADGĪTĀ. (1) **Introduction.**

Article 'Bhagavadgītā' in *E.R.E.* Also Introduction of No. 57.

(2) **Translations.**

57. *The Bhagavadgītā.* Translated by L. D. Barnett, M.A., Litt.D. Dent & Co. 2*s*. 6*d*.

58. *The Bhagavadgītā.* Sanskrit text and English translation. By Mrs. Besant. Madras: Natesan. As. 2.

XII. THE PURĀṆAS. (1) **Introduction.**

Chap. XVI of No. 2, and pages 299–301 of No. 6. See also Introduction to No. 59.

(2) **Translations.**

59. *Vishṇu Purāṇa.* Introduction and translation by Prof. H. H. Wilson. Murray. Out of print.

60. *Mārkaṇḍeya-Purāṇa.* By F. E. Pargiter. Calcutta: The Asiatic Society. 15*s*.

61. *Garuḍa Purāṇa Sāroddhāra.* Translated by Wood and Subrahmanyam. Allahabad: Pāṇini Office. Rs. 3 as. 8.

62. *Bhāgavata Purāṇa.* Texte sanscrit et traduction française par E. Burnouf. 4 vols. Paris.

63. *The Vishṇu, Agni, Mārkaṇḍeya, Garuḍa, and Bhāgavata Purāṇas.* Translated by M. N. Dutt. Calcutta: Elysium Press.

XIII. THE SAṀHITĀS, ĀGAMAS, AND TANTRAS.

For the Vishṇuite Saṁhitās see *J.R.A.S.*, October, 1911; for the Śaiva Āgamas see No. 76 below; and for the Tantras, pp. 489–94 of No. 2.

64. *Mahānirvāṇa Tantra.* Translated by M. N. Dutt. Calcutta: Elysium Press.

XIV. THE BHAKTI SECTS AND THEIR MODERN REVIVAL.

(*a*) **General.**

Pages 1–100 of No. 4, or Chaps. V and VI of No. 79, along with the article 'Bhakti Mārga' in *E.R.E.* and Chap. XI of No. 5, will suffice as a general introduction to Vaishṇavism. Nos. 68 and 70 give information about the division of Rāmānuja's people into two sects. In order to realize how the philosophy of Rāmānuja worked itself out in practice, No. 67 should be read. Chap. XIV of No. 7 gives a good introduction to the northern sects. For Śaivism see No. 76 and the introductory pages of No. 77. Nos. 67, 68, 74, 76, are well worth notice as examples of the better type of literature produced by the revival of Hinduism. For Neo-Kṛishṇa books see No. 119, Appendix.

65. *The Bhakti Sūtra of Śāṇḍilya.* Translated by Cowell. Calcutta : Asiatic Society. Out of print.

(*b*) The Sect of Rāmānuja. (1) Biographies.

66. *The Holy Lives of the Āzhvārs.* By A. Govindāchārya Svāmī. Mysore : G.T.A. Press. Re. 1 as. 8.

Uncritical, yet informing.

67. *Life of Rāmānuja.* By A. Govindāchārya Svāmī. Madras : S. Murthy & Co. Rs. 2 as. 12.

This is a translation of an ancient Tamil biography of the philosopher. It is a most revealing book.

68. *The Vaishṇavite Reformers of India* (seven biographies). By Rājāgopāla Chāriar. Madras : Natesan. Re. 1.

(2) System.

See No. 46.

69. *The Teachings of the Vedānta according to Rāmānuja.* By V. A. Sukhtankar. Vienna : Holzhausen.

70. *The Artha-Pañchaka of Piḷḷai Lokāchārya.* Translated by A. Govindāchārya Svāmī. Reprinted from *J.R.A.S.*, July, 1910.

(*c*) Rāmānanda and Tulsī Dās.

Pages 26–37 of No. 4; pages 147–8 of No. 79; page cxxiv of No 72, and pages 418–20 of No. 5. For Tulsī Dās's great poem see No. 37.

(*d*) Kabīr.

71. *Kabīr and the Kabīrpanth.* By the Rev. G. H. Westcott, M.A., Bishop of Lucknow. Cawnpore : Mission Press. Re. 1 as. 8.

(*e*) The Sikhs.

See pages 374–9 of No. 7, or pages 161–78 of No. 79, or Carpenter's article in the *Hibbert Journal* for October, 1911.

72. *The Ādi Granth.* Translated by Dr. Ernest Trumpp. W. H. Allen & Co. 63*s.*

73. *The Sikh Religion*: a translation of the *Granth*, with lives of the Gurus. By M. A. Macauliffe. 6 vols. Clarendon Press. 63*s.* net.

(*f*) Mādhvism.

74. *The Life and Teachings of Śrī Madhvāchāryar.* By C. M. Padmanābha Chār, B.A., B.L. Published by the author at Coimbatore. Rs. 3.

Written by a Mādhva, yet reasonable on the whole, and full of information.

For Mādhva's philosophy, see No. 48.

(*g*) **Tukārām.**

75. *The Poems of Tukārām.* Translated and re-arranged by J. Nelson Fraser, M.A., and K. B. Marathe, B.A., LL.B. Christian Literature Society. (Rs. 2 as. 8.) 3*s.* 9*d.*

(*h*) **Vallabhāchārya and Chaitanya.**

Pages 60–9 and 79–91 of No. 4, along with pages 134–7 of No. 79.

(*i*) **Śaivism.**

76. *Studies in Śaiva-Siddhānta.* By J. M. Nallasvāmi Pillai, B.A., B.L. Meykandan Press, Madras. Rs. 3.

Not absolutely reliable, but full of good material.

77. *The Tiruvāśagam of Māṇikka Vāśagar.* By G. U. Pope. Introduction, text, translation. Clarendon Press. 21*s.* net.

For the Śaiva philosophical system, see No. 47.

XV. Hinduism as lived To-day.

No. 79 gives the best survey; but the student who wishes to obtain from Indian sources a vivid impression of the real character of Hinduism even at its best should read No. 67. For Hindu law see Nos. 38 and 39.

78. *The Hindu at Home.* By the Rev. J. E. Padfield, B.D. Madras: S.P.C.K. Out of print.

Describes vividly the superstitions of Southern India.

79. *Brāhmanism and Hindūism.* By Sir Monier Monier-Williams, K.C.I.E., D.C.L., M.A. Murray. Out of print.

This book gives in clear and accurate form the details of Hindu worship and observance.

80. *Imperial Gazetteer of India*, vol. i. Clarendon Press. 6*s.* net.

Deals with India and its resources, ethnology, caste, languages, religions, and statistics.

81. *The Village Deities of Southern India.* By the Bishop of Madras. Government Press, Madras. 1*s.* 3*d.*

XVI. The Modern Samājes, &c.

The article 'Brāhma Samāj' in *E.R.E.* will introduce the student to the theistic movement in Bengal. If that work is not available, a good summary of the history down to 1884 may be found in pages 475 to 528 of No. 79; or No. 82 may be used. The best account of the Ārya Samāj is also in *E.R.E.* The serious student had better read No. 89 also, as it is by the founder, and contains his autobiography.

82. *The Brāhma Samāj and other Modern Eclectic Systems of Religion in India.* Christian Literature Society. (As. 3.) 6*d.*

83. *Biographical Essays.* By Max Müller. Longmans. 5*s.*

Contains brief lives of Rām Mohan Ray, Keshab Chandra Sen, Dayānanda Sarasvatī, Colebrooke the Sanskrit scholar, and others.

84. *The Life and Letters of Rāja Rām Mohan Ray.* By Sophia Dobson Collet. Published privately in 1900 at 2*s.* 6*d.*

85. *The Autobiography of Maharshi Devendranāth Tagore.* Translated from the original Bengali by Satyendranath Tagore and Indira Devi. Calcutta: Lahīri & Co. Rs. 2 as. 8.

86. *Lectures in India.* By Keshab Chandra Sen. 2 vols. Cassell. Each vol. 5*s.* net.

87. *The Life and Teachings of Keshab Chandra Sen.* By Pratāp Chandra Mozoomdar. Calcutta: Baptist Mission Press.

A full and fairly accurate account of the life.

88. *The Oriental Christ.* By Pratāp Chandra Mozoomdar. Boston: Ellis. 6*s.* 6*d.*

A striking work from an advanced Brāhma position.

89. *Dayānanda Sarasvatī's Satyārtha Prakash in English.* Translated from the original Hindī by Durgā Prasād. Lahore: Vir'anand Press. Rs. 2 as. 4.

The basis of the teaching of the Ārya Samāj.

90. *Rāmakṛishṇa, His Life and Sayings.* By Max Müller. Longmans. 5*s.*

91. *Svāmī Vivekānanda, a Collection of his Speeches and Writings.* Madras: Natesan. Rs. 2.

XVII. BUDDHISM.

(1) General Introduction.

92. *Buddhism as a Religion.* By H. Hackmann. Probsthain. 6*s.* net.

Gives a life of the Buddha, a sketch of his doctrine and the historical development of Buddhism and a description of the religion as it exists in the various Buddhist lands to-day.

(2) Early Buddhism.

93. *Buddhist India.* By T. W. Rhys Davids. Fisher Unwin. 5*s.*

Gives a vivid picture of the historical conditions in which Buddhism arose.

94. *Buddha.* By Dr. Hermann Oldenberg. Williams & Norgate. 18*s.*

A critical study of Buddha's life and doctrine and of his monastic order.

95. *Manual of Indian Buddhism.* By H. Kern. *Grundriss.* 8*s.* 6*d.*
A detailed survey of early Buddhism.

96. *Buddhism: its History and Literature.* By T. W. Rhys Davids. Putnam's Sons. 6*s.*

97. *Buddhism in Translations.* By H. C. Warren. Harvard Oriental Series. Ginn & Co. 5*s.* net.

A very fine selection of translations illustrating the teaching of early Buddhism.

98. Vols. x, xi, xiii, xvii, xx of the *S.B.E.* give translations of selected texts from each of the Piṭakas.

99. *Buddhism, Primitive and Present, in Magadha, and in Ceylon.* By the Bishop of Calcutta. Longmans. 10*s.* 6*d.* net.

100. *The Legend of Gaudama.* By Bishop Bigandet. Trübner. 21*s.*
Forms a most interesting introduction to Burmese Buddhism.

(3) Mahāyāna Buddhism.

101. Vols. xxi, xxxv, xxxvi, and xlix of the *S.B.E.* contain Mahāyāna texts, and form the best introduction to the Mahāyāna.

102. *Aśvaghosha's Awakening of Faith in the Mahāyāna.* Translated by T. Suzuki. Chicago. 5*s.* net.

103. *The Path of Light*, a Translation of Śānti-deva's *Bodhicharyāvatāra.* By L. D. Barnett, M.A., D.D. Murray. 2*s.* net.

104. *Le Lalita Vistara.* Traduit par P. E. Foucaux. Paris: Ernest Leroux. 15 fr.

105. *A Catalogue of the Chinese Buddhist Tripiṭaka.* By Bunyiu Nanjio. Clarendon Press. 30*s.* net.
Gives in convenient form a conspectus of the Mahāyāna canon.

(4) Tāntric Buddhism.

106. *The Buddhism of Tibet.* By Col. I. A. Waddell. W. H. Allen. 31*s.* 6*d.*

107. *The Life of the Buddha and the Early History of his Order.* From Tibetan sources. By W. W. Rockhill. Trübner. 9*s.*

108. *Udānavarga.* By W. W. Rockhill. Trübner. 9*s.*

XVIII. Jainism.

109. *The Indian Sect of the Jainas.* By J. G. Bühler. Luzac. 3*s.* 6*d.*

110. *Notes on Modern Jainism.* By Mrs. Sinclair Stevenson. Oxford: Blackwell. 1*s.* 6*d.* net.

111. *Jaina Sūtras.* Translated by Hermann Jacobi. *S.B.E.*, vols. xxii and xlv. 16*s.* net and 12*s.* 6*d.* net.

XIX. Hinduism and Christianity.

112. *The Challenge of the Non-Christian Religions.* A reprint of the concluding chapter of Commission IV of the World Missionary Conference. Oliphant: Anderson & Ferrier. *6d.* net.

113. *Dialogues on Indian Philosophy.* By the late Rev. K. M. Bannerjea. Christian Literature Society. (Re. 1 as. 10.) *2s. 6d.*

114. *A Mirror of the Hindu Philosophical Systems.* By Nehemiah Nīlakaṇṭha Śāstrī Goreh, translated from the original Hindī by Fitz-Edward Hall, D.C.L. Christian Literature Society. (Re. 1 as. 10.) *2s 6d.*

Nos. 113 and 114 are classic treatises by Brāhman converts of high scholarly attainments, but they are a little too far advanced for the beginner, and they lack the historic point of view.

115. *The High Caste Hindu Woman.* By Paṇḍitā Rāmabai. Revell. *2s. 6d.* net.

A striking volume by a lady who was born a Hindu, and has had such experience as scarcely any other woman in India has had.

116. *Things As They Are.* By Amy Wilson-Carmichael. Morgan & Scott. Paper, *1s. 6d.* net.

A very vivid yet altogether trustworthy picture of the darker side of Hinduism in South India.

117. *The Higher Hinduism in Relation to Christianity.* By the Rev. T. E. Slater. Elliot Stock. *2s. 6d.*

118. *Karma and Redemption.* By A. G. Hogg, M.A. Christian Literature Society. (As. 6.) *1s.*

This is a most original piece of thinking on the subject of transmigration and karma.

119. *Gītā and Gospel.* By J. N. Farquhar, M.A. Christian Literature Society. (As. 6.) *9d.*

120. *India's Problem: Kṛishṇa or Christ.* By John P. Jones, D.D. Revell. *5s.* net.

121. *The Desire of India.* By S. K. Datta, B.A., M.B., Ch.B. London: Young People's Missionary Movement. *2s.* net.

Written for Mission Study. Gives a vivid picture of the people of India to-day, and a convincing statement of their need of Christ.

122. *An Interpretation of India's Religious History.* By the Rev. R. A. Hume, D.D. Revell. *3s. 6d.*

INDEX